A
PICTORIAL HISTORY
OF CIVIL WAR ERA
MUSICAL INSTRUMENTS
& MILITARY BANDS

A
PICTORIAL HISTORY
OF CIVIL WAR ERA
MUSICAL INSTRUMENTS
& MILITARY BANDS

The New Haven (Connecticut) Brass Band. Drawn and painted by George Edwards Candee in 1851. This 15-piece brass band, which appears to be marching in a firemen's parade, is equipped with OTS and upright saxhorns. Courtesy of the New York State Historical Association, Coopertown, N.Y.

By Robert Garofalo & Mark Elrod

PICTORIAL HISTORIES PUBLISHING COMPANY
CHARLESTON, WEST VIRGINIA

LIBRARY OF CONGRESS
CATALOG CARD NUMBER 85-60321

ISBN 0-933126-60-3

First Printing   April 1985
Second Printing   April 1987

Typography: Arrow Graphics & Typography
Layout: Stan Cohen
Cover Graphics: Allen Woodard
Cover Photo: G. Thaddeus Jones
E-flat alto saxhorn and rope tension eagle drum
from the Mark Elrod and Fred Benkovic Collections

PICTORIAL HISTORIES PUBLISHING COMPANY
4103 Virginia Avenue S.E., Charleston, West Virginia 25304

FOREWORD

This publication is an outgrowth of Heritage Americana, Inc., a research-performance project whose objective is the study of nineteenth century Americana brass bands—their history, instruments, literature, and performance practices. Heritage Americana aims to stimulate an interest in the music and instruments of a unique musical era in American social and cultural history, and to instill a sense of pride and patriotism in our national heritage.

This book portrays both in pictures and in narrative the colorful history of Civil War era military bands and musical instruments. Most of the approximately 200 photographs that appear in the book have never been published before. Nearly half of the photographs are of musical instruments made in America between 1840 and 1870. More than 40 early instrument makers are represented. Unless noted otherwise in the captions, instruments are shown with original or period equipment (mouthpieces, cases, sticks, etc.). Except for cymbals, instrument dimensions are not given because it was not possible to get consistent measurements for all instruments. To date instruments, the following sources were used: manufacturers' catalogues and advertisements, trade journals and music directories, and indexes of musical instruments. Instruments which included the address as well as the name of the maker could, in most instances, be fairly accurately dated with knowledge of the dates and location of the maker's business. A useful source for this information was an index of *Early American Makers of Woodwind and Brass Musical Instruments* recently compiled by Dr. Robert Eliason, Curator of Musical Instruments at the Henry Ford Museum, Dearborn, Michigan. Eliason's unpublished index, which was intended to be used by collectors, dealers, and museum curators, includes detailed information about American firms beginning business before 1875.

Photography had not yet been invented when the American brass band movement began in the mid-1830s. (Daguerreotypy, the first successful photographic process, was introduced in Europe in 1839). We used copies of lithographs, paintings, prints, and piano sheet music covers to depict early bands and bandsmen. Actual photographs of these subjects begin to appear in the 1850s; however, the images of some early photographs are unclear. We reluctantly had to reject an interesting photograph of a brass band taken around 1850 because it would not reproduce satisfactorily. The photograph depicts 11 boys playing on keyed bugles, ophicleides, an E-flat trumpet, a trombone, a clarinet, and a large brass drum. Mixed instrumentation of this type was typical of early brass bands. Unfortunately, very few photographs of these bands exist.

Photography developed rapidly in the 1850s. By 1861, several types of photographic techniques were in use. We had no problems finding good photographs of Civil War bands and bandsmen. Most photographs were reproduced exactly as we received them. In a few instances, however, we corrected the image reversal to properly depict some important detail in a picture. (Most early photographic processes produced reversed images.)

To date photographs of bands and bandsmen, we examined the photo backmarks and considered the types of photography used; we also looked carefully at the instruments and uniforms. For example, we were able to date the photograph of Gilmore's Band by comparing the headgear worn by the militia unit pictured with the band with the dress caps illustrated and described in Edgar M. Howell's *United States Army Headgear 1855-1902* (Washinton, D.C.: Smithsonian Institution Press, 1975). The headgear worn by the militiamen was part of the 1872 regulation uniform. Of course, for some photographs we relied on the judgements of knowledgeable collectors who provided the photographs.

This book includes a record sampler with examples of Union and Confederate band music played on period instruments. Most of the instruments used in the recording are illustrated in the book. The selections demonstrate the pleasing sound of the instruments and the emotional power of the music, both of which sustained the development of brass bands in this country before, during, and after the Civil War.

ACKNOWLEDGMENTS

This book would not have been possible without the cooperation of many individuals, museums, libraries, and historical associations whose names appear in the photo credits. We thank all of them for their help. A special thank you is extended to the following people for their assistance. Bruce Bazelon, Curator of the William Penn Memorial Museum, Harrisburg, Pennsylvania, provided documentation for several of the drums and related photographs included in chapter three. Jon Newsom, Assistant Chief of the Music Division of the Library of Congress, provided photographs of bands from the Prints and Photographs Division, and he researched anecdotal information that was used with the photos. Jon Hall of Portland, Maine, researched information on the history of bands and bandsmen from Maine; he also provided excellent photographs of musical instruments from his collection. Paul Maybery of St. Paul, Minnesota, provided historical information about Minnesota bands. Fred Benkovic of Wauwastosa, Wisconsin, provided photographs and historical information for many of the brass and percussion instruments. (Benkovic's instrument collection is one of the largest and most interesting private holdings of its kind in the country.) Several of the drums illustrated in chapter three were restored by Benkovic, who is an acknowledged expert in that field.

The following individuals deserve special recognition because they contributed excellent photographs that enriched the book: Kurt Stein (early lithographs, paintings, and piano sheet music covers), Robert Hazen (bands and bandsmen), Henry Deeks (Patrick Gilmore and his band), and George Carroll (color photographs of rope tension drums).

Although the name G. Thaddeus Jones seldom appears in the credits, his expert photography is revealed on almost every page of the book. Dr. Jones, who is Professor Emeritus of the School of Music, The Catholic University of America, Washington, D.C., photographed all of the instruments from the Elrod, Garofalo, and Jack Silver collections, and reproduced many of the photographs of bands and bandsmen.

We are greatly indebted to Mr. George Wheelock of Bowie, Maryland, who provided editorial assistance. George has been associated with Heritage Americana since its establishment in 1978. His knowledge of music and his expertise as a college English professor made him the ideal person to consult for manuscript revisions. His suggestions for improvement appear throughout the book.

Finally, we wish to thank our publisher, Mr. Stan Cohen, for his support, encouragement, and patience during the year and a half that the book was in preparation.

Robert Garofalo and Mark Elrod
Washington, D.C.

CONTENTS

In memory of John Elrod (1910-1983) whose love of music inspired the writing of this book.

CHAPTER ONE
EARLY BRASS BAND INSTRUMENTS

Military bands of the Union and Confederate armies were a noteworthy part of the American brass band movement. This movement, which flourished for more than a half century (beginning in the mid-1830s), depended upon the development and refinement of keyed and valved brass instruments.[1]

Civil War military bands were, with few exceptions, composed entirely of brass and percussion instruments. This was a nineteenth century phenomenon made possible by the development of brass instruments which could easily play the entire musical scale. Earlier military bands used clarinets and oboes for melodic parts because they were among the few soprano wind instruments not restricted in melodic capability.

KEYED BUGLES AND OPHICLEIDES

The gradual movement toward all-brass bands in America began around 1815 with the introduction into this country of the keyed bugle or Royal Kent bugle.[2] This instrument has a conically shaped bore (the brass tube is a continuously tapered cone from the lead pipe to the bell) with side holes and keys that are similar to those of the saxophone. The keyed bugle was the first brass instrument that could satisfactorily produce diatonic and chromatic tones,[3] and it rapidly replaced the clarinet as the leading melodic voice in American bands.[4]

Considering the practice of building instruments in families, it is not surprising to find that the invention of the keyed bugle soon inspired the creation of larger keyed brasses that could extend the playing range downward. The Parisian instrument maker Halary (Jean-Hilaire Aste) was the first to build (in 1817) and patent (in 1821) an entire family of keyed brass instruments that he named ophicleides.[5] Early ophicleides were built in six sizes from altos (called quinticlaves) to contrabasses.

Keyed bugles and ophicleides became increasingly popular with American bandmen in the 1820s and 1830s. Their greater carrying power made them preferable to woodwinds for open air performances. Although keyed brass instruments laid the foundation for the development of brass bands in the United States, they were soon replaced by improved brass instruments with valves. The change occurred in the 1840s for low brasses, with several types of valved instruments replacing the ophicleide. The keyed

bugle lost favor in the 1850s when it became clear that the newer valved instruments were much easier to play and produced a more even tone quality.

E-flat keyed bugle in form fitted case. Marked "Made for E.G. Wright by Allen & Co., Boston," c. 1855. Sterling silver with 11 box mounted keys. Fred Benkovic Collection. The inscription on the bell of the presentation instrument reads: "Thomas B. Harris, Xenia, Ohio."

(1) Although England experienced a similar brass band movement in the nineteenth century, there were fundamental differences between the American and British bands. The instruments, instrumentation, and literature were different. British brass bands were predominantly amateur organizations, whereas American bands were both amateur and professional. American brass bands were gradually replaced by bands using woodwind and brass instruments toward the end of the nineteenth century, but British brass bands have had a continuous, unbroken tradition of performance and national competition to the present day.

(2) The keyed bugle was invented by Joseph Haliday of Dublin, Ireland, and patented by him in 1810 (British Patent No. 3334). Haliday was director of the Cavan Militia band and an accomplished performer on the instrument. Although most sources state that Haliday named his instrument in honor of the Duke of Kent who had heard him perform on the instrument and expressed admiration of it, recent research seems to refute that claim. See Ralph Dudgeon, "Joseph Haliday, Inventor of the Keyed Bugle," *Journal of the American Musical Instrument Society*, Vol. IX, 1983, pp. 53-67.

(3) Diatonic tones are the notes of the standard major and minor scales; chromatic tones are the notes of the chromatic scale which consist entirely of half steps (semitones).

VALVED BRASSES

The invention of the first successful valve for brass instruments is generally attributed to Heinrich Stoelzel and Freiderich Bluhmel, two Berlin musicians who patented their design in 1818.[6] In the decades immediately following the introduction of the "Stoelzel valve," numerous valve systems were devised in Europe, England, and America.

The 1830s were unusually productive in the creation of valve designs with lasting influence on the development of brass instruments. Most important among these were the Vienna twin-piston valve (patented by Leopold Uhlmann in 1830), the "Rad-Maschine" (a rotary-action valve designed by Joseph Riedl of Vienna and patented in 1832), the Berliner "pumpen" valve (a piston design patented by Wilhelm Wieprecht and J.G. Moritz in Prussia in 1835), and the Perinet valve (a piston valve named after the Parisian instrument maker who introduced it in 1839).

To appreciate the significance of these and other valve inventions, it is important to understand how early brass instruments functioned. A natural trumpet or horn, one without keys or valves, could only produce a limited series of ascending tones. The performer accomplished this by increasing lip tension at the instrument's mouthpiece. The interval arrangement of the tones that could be played—octave, fifth, fourth, major third, minor third, and so on—always remained the same no matter what the fundamental pitch of the instrument. A natural trumpet in D, for example, could only produce an overtone series based on its fundamental note D. Therefore, trumpet and horn players were greatly handicapped in their ability to play melodic passages. What was needed was a mechanism whereby a player could rapidly fill in the gaps in the natural overtone series. The valve was that mechanism.

Most early valve brass instruments had only two valves. The first valve lowered any natural open tone by one semitone, the second valve by two semitones. When the third valve was added around 1825 (it lowered any open tone by three semitones), it became possible to play all notes of the chromatic scale. By using the valves singly or in combination, the natural tones of a brass instrument could be lowered by one to six semitones. Thus, the gaps between the open tones could be filled in (except for the bottom interval). Although three-valved instruments were fairly common by the late 1830s, neither the number nor the arrangement of valves became standardized before the middle of the nineteenth century.

Valve mechanisms can be grouped into two basic types—piston and rotary valves. The piston valve has an up and down motion. When the valve is in the up position, the wind passes directly through the instrument's main tube. When engaged, the valve redirects the wind through an additional short length of tubing before it is allowed to re-enter the main tube. With the

---

(4) Early nineteenth century American and European bands consisted of pairs of clarinets, oboes, horns, and bassoons, with the possible addition of one or more of the following instruments: trumpet (without keys or valves), flute, trombone, serpent, and percussion (triangle, Turkish crescent, cymbals, drums).

(5) The name "ophicleide" is derived from two Greek words—*ophis* (a serpent) and *kleis* (a cover or stopper). Although ophicleide literally means keyed serpent it has little in common with the earlier bass instrument called "serpent."

(6) For a four-part scholarly treatise on the early history of valves based on surviving documents of the Royal Prussian Technical Delegation, see Herbert Heyde, "Zur Fruhgeschichte der Ventrile in Deutschland (1814-1833)," *Brass Bulletin*, Vols. XXIV-XXVII, 1978-79.

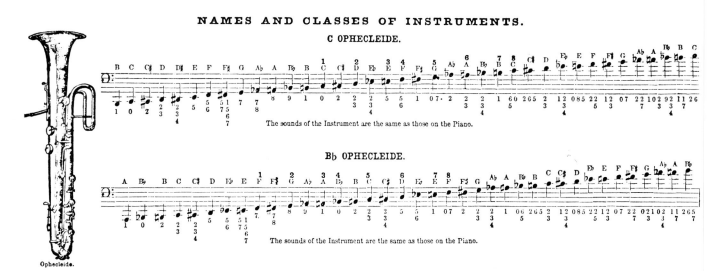

Bass ophicleide fingering charts from *Dodworth's Brass Band School* (1853).

rotary valve the wind flow is controlled by a revolving cylinder. The rotation of the cylinder is controlled by a key or lever that is connected to the rotor by either string or mechanical linkage.

CORNETS AND SAXHORNS

From c. 1825 to c. 1845, instrument makers in different countries constructed brass instruments with unusual shapes and various types and numbers of valves. Some makers even built hybrid instruments that combined both valves and keys. Although most of these instruments eventually proved to be unsatisfactory, two very successful valve brass instruments were created during this period of great experimentation—the cornet and the saxhorn. These were to play a major role in military bands of the Civil War.

The cornet was created around 1825 when French instrument makers added piston valves to the post horn. Because the tube bore of the cornet was more conical in shape that that of the trumpet, the instrument produced a sweet, mellow tone. The cornet's pleasing sound and ease of execution guaranteed its popularity as a solo and melodic brass instrument in bands from the 1840s to the present day.

Larger valved brass instruments—alto, tenor, baritone, and bass horns—were developed by European makers beginning in the late 1820s. Later, in the early 1840s, a complete family (soprano to bass) of homogeneous valved bugles or saxhorns was created. Saxhorns were named after their creator, Adolphe Sax, the well-known Franco-Belgian instrument maker and inventor (who also developed saxophones, a family of woodwind instruments).

Saxhorns have fairly large bores (relative to their length) which expand rapidly in the last section; the bells flare only moderately. Because the tube bores of saxhorns are predominantly conical, the instruments produce a soft, mellow sound that blends well together. They have sufficient carrying power to be heard out of doors. Their intonation, while not perfect, is relatively accurate. The instruments are comparatively easy to play. The combination of these qualities made saxhorns very popular.

Early saxhorns were built in the bell upright design and had three stout Berliner "pumpen" valves. Neither the bell design nor the valve type were original ideas with Sax. However, it was his technical knowledge and skilled craftsmanship in applying existing ideas that allowed him to create a superior family of valve brass instruments that quickly gained wide acceptance in Great Britain and America.

To fully appreciate the impact the saxhorns and cornets had on the instrumentation of brass bands in this

Lithograph showing an early brass band and militia regiment marching near Henry Prentiss' music store, 52 Court Street, Boston, c. 1838. Courtesy of Kurt Stein.

country, it is necessary to understand the favorable circumstances that surrounded their introduction.

The beginning of the brass band era in America is generally considered to be 1835, the year in which the first all-brass bands were established in this country. These early bands employed a variety of brass instruments in their instrumentation—keyed bugles, ophicleides, French horns (without valves), trumpets, post horns, trombones, and so on. This heterogeneous instrumentation probably caused severe problems of balance, blend, and intonation. Also, it must have been difficult for bandleaders to train amateurs for their bands, given the different techniques required to play the instruments. Troublesome as these factors may have been, they did not deter communities from organizing town bands with increasing frequency in the 1840s as the brass band phenomenon continued to gather momentum. According to Jon Newsom of the Library of Congress: "Interest in the formation of amateur brass bands was growing at such a rate that by the mid-1850s it had reached the proportions of a significant popular movement."[7]

The proliferation of brass bands in this country created a strong demand for new and improved instruments. Saxhorns, cornets, and similarly designed valved brass instruments, whether imported or American made, satisfactorily fulfilled the demand.

YANKEE INGENUITY

Until recently, little was known about the contributions Americans made to the development of chro-

(7) "The American Brass Band Movement," *The Quarterly Journal of the Library of Congress* (Spring, 1979), p. 123.

maticized brass instruments. Nor was it known that this country had had a thriving brass instrument industry by the middle of the nineteenth century. Thanks to the research and publications of Dr. Robert Eliason, Curator of Musical Instruments at the Henry Ford Museum, we now know that there were dozens of early American craftsmen who were making good quality instruments for amateur and professional bands in this country prior to the Civil War.[8]

In two of his excellent books,[9] Eliason documents the contrubtions of five Yankee craftsmen whose work significantly advanced the development of brass instruments in the nineteenth century—Samuel Graves, Thomas D. Paine, J. Lathrop Allen, Elbridge G. Wright, and Isaac Fiske. According to Eliason, Graves' manufactory was the earliest and most important in terms of production, size, and variety of instruments. Concerning the other four makers, Eliason writes:

> Paine was the first to produce rotary valves with string linkage—a combination which dominated American production for nearly half a century and is still in use on modern French horns. J. Lathrop Allen was distinguished for his invention of the Allen valve, [a quick-action rotary valve that was] popular among American players until late in the century. E.G. Wright carried the development of the key bugle to its zenith and was famous for the beautiful presentation instruments he made of silver and gold. Isaac Fiske was noted for his work on eliminating restriction in the bore of brasses and for attempts to provide the cornet with lighter, quicker valve action.[10]

American made brass instruments were handcrafted in shops located in the Northeast. Although Boston was the main center of instrument making activity, New York and Philadelphia had prosperous manufacturing establishments as did several small towns in New England. Most of the brass instruments illustrated in this book were made at these locations between 1840 and 1870; they give silent testimony to the quality of Yankee ingenuity and workmanship during the mid-nineteenth century.

---

(8) Commenting on the selection of a good brass instrument in the early 1850s, Allen Dodworth wrote: "It is conceded by nearly all, that the finest quality of instruments are now made here, by our American manufacturers." *Dodworth's Brass Band School* (New York: H.B. Dodworth & Co., 1853), p. 12.

(9) Robert Eliason, *Graves & Company: Musical Instrument Makers* (Dearborn, Michigan: The Edison Institute, 1975); and *Early American Brass Makers* (Nashville, Tennessee: The Brass Press, 1981).

(10) *Early American Brass Makers*, p. 3.

KEYED BRASSES

Keyed bugle in E-flat. Made by Graves & Co., Winchester, N.H., c. 1845. Copper with German silver trim and 10 box mounted keys. Elrod Collection.

E-flat key bugler, c. 1860. His instrument appears to have 9 keys with box mounts. Courtesy of Robert Hazen.

Keyed bugle in E-flat. Marked "E.G. Wright Maker, No. 8 Bromfield St., Boston," c. 1847. Copper with 10 silver keys mounted with footposts and screws. Elrod Collection.

Keyed bugle in B-flat. Made by J. Keats for Graves & Co., Winchester, N.H., c. 1840. Copper with brass trim and seven box mounted keys. Elrod Collection. The period mouthpiece in the "pigtail" lead pipe is not original equipment.

Close up of the decorative strips used by Wright to cover the seams of his keyed bugle.

Keyed bugle in E-flat. Marked "Made by Graves & Co., Boston," c. 1850s. German silver with 12 keys mounted with footposts and screws. Kurt Stein Collection. This presentation bugle has a telescopic tuning shank in the lead pipe which is used to adjust the overall pitch of the instrument.

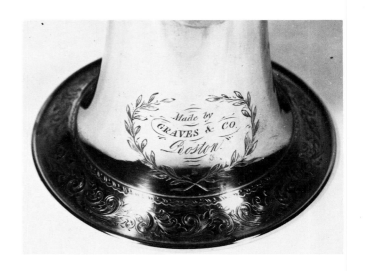

Alto ophicleide (quinticlave) in E-flat. Made by Graves & Co., Winchester, N.H., c. 1840s. Brass with 10 keys. From the Collections of the Henry Ford Museum and Greenfield Village, Dearborn, Michigan.

CHAPTER TWO
CIVIL WAR ERA BRASS INSTRUMENTS

When hostilities broke out between the North and South in the spring of 1861, America was ready to provide Union and Confederate volunteer regiments with military bands that were needed to inspire patriotism and fighting spirit. Militia and community bands were flourishing in towns and cities throughout the country. Large numbers of amateurs were experienced at playing instruments, and professional band musicians were at an all time high. Music publishing and merchandising businesses were prospering. American instrument manufacturers were turning out products that were equal to or better than those of their European competitors. Thus, the stage was set for the cli-

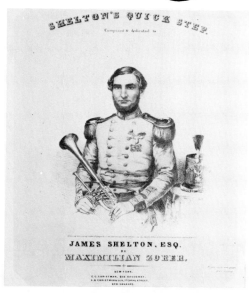

"Shelton's Quick Step. Composed and dedicated to James Shelton, Esq., by Maximilian Zorer" (New York: C.G. Christman, 1852). Shelton, a professional cornetist and bandleader in New York City, is shown here with his usual combination saxhorn which has valves and keys. The Henry Ford Museum houses the only known specimen that is similar to the one pictured here (see below). Courtesy of Kurt Stein.

Valve and key soprano saxhorn in E-flat. Made by E.G. Wright, Boston, c. 1853. German silver with three string rotary valves and five keys. From the Collections of the Henry Ford Museum and Greenfield Village, Dearborn, Michigan. In the early 1850s, when the cornet was seriously challenging the supremacy of the keyed bugle, Wright began making soprano brass instruments with both rotary valves and keys in an attempt to combine the best of both systems. Allen Dodworth, who liked the new instruments, wrote in his *Brass Band School* of 1853 that "they combine the fullness of tone in the lower notes peculiar to valve instruments with the greater ease of facility of the upper notes which is peculiar to keyed instruments." Despite the advantages, the combination design was not widely accepted.

Early brass instrument mouthpieces: E-flat and B-flat cornet and saxhorn, E-flat alto horn, B-flat tenor horn or baritone, and E-flat bass. Most period mouthpieces were made of brass or German silver; however, a few pewter specimens and even nickel plated ones have been found.

mactic development of the brass band movement. The war gave a tremendous impetus to the movement.

CLASSIFICATIONS

Civil War valved brass instruments can be classified into four general categories which are determined by the direction of the bell and the shape of the instrument. They are bell front, upright, circular, and over the shoulder. In addition to the four shapes, the instruments can be subclassified according to the type of valve mechanism used. The two most common valve types were the American string linkage rotary valve (top or side action) and the durable Berliner piston valve. The latter valve type was relatively inexpensive to produce and was less likely to cause mechanical problems in the field.

Brass and German silver were the main materials used in Civil War horns. Because the metal was thin and quite soft, numerous intonation problems occurred with changes in humidity, temperature, and exposure to sunlight or rain. However, brass instruments were still a great improvement over the more fragile woodwind instruments in military bands because they could better withstand the rigors of outdoor use.

The fundamental tuning frequencies of Civil War era brass instruments vary considerably. Most are sharp compared to the modern standard pitch, but they vary enough in degree of sharpness that some instruments cannot be tuned to agree with others of the period. Electronic measurements of the overall tuning frequencies of more than 40 instruments showed a substantial variation. Because there was no standard tuning frequency to guide manufacturers, their choices varied; therefore, it was helpful for a band to have a matched set of instruments from the same

The cups of period mouthpieces have a deep, funnel shape, and the inner rims are sharply angled. The design, which is similar to the one used for modern French horn mouthpieces, enhances the warm, mellow tone quality of early cornets and saxhorns.

firm. (Several bands pictured in this book appear to have matched sets of instruments.)

Civil War horns have several intonation flaws that occur when valves are used. Skilled bandsmen undoubtedly used alternate fingering and lipping techniques to play problem notes in tune. Our experiences with period instruments have shown that it is easy to lip a pitch in tune because the old horns have wide, conical bores. Civil War horns do not have valve slide triggers and rings or other intonation-improving devices that are commonly found on modern brass instruments. Nor do they have water keys. There was no easy method whereby a musician could empty collected moisture out of his instrument.

OVER THE SHOULDER SAXHORNS

The style of brass instrument most often associated with Civil War bands was the over the shoulder saxhorn, or OTS saxhorn for short. Its distinguishing characteristic was the direction of the bell, which was pointed to the rear to direct the sound of the music to the troops marching behind the band. Although the origin of the over the shoulder design is obscure, it is believed that such instruments were first used in this country by the Dodworth Brass Band of New York City in the late 1830s. The design is often attributed to Thomas Dodworth and his two sons Allen and Harvey; however, to date no patent has been found to document that fact.[1]

The naming of saxhorns and other instruments of the period was often inconsistent. The terms *saxhorn* and *cornet* were indiscriminately used to refer to a wide variety of conically bored soprano brass instruments with differing shapes and valve mechanisms. By 1860 the term *cornet* had assumed a generic meaning and was generally understood to refer to "any soprano valved brass instrument that could be used to play the melodic part, rather than to one particular type of instrument."[2] We have opted to use the term *cornet* for all bell front and circular valve brass instruments and *saxhorn* for upright and OTS designs. We recognize the difficulty with this nomenclature, as some bell front instruments have extremely wide conical bores that are similar in shape to the tubing of keyed bugles and thus are true saxhorns (or "flugelhorns" as they are called in German).

SOUND AND BALANCE

Civil War era bands frequently played on brass instruments whose bells pointed in three different directions: forward (bell front cornets), upward (circular cornets and upright saxhorns), and backward (OTS saxhorns). This peculiar situation undoubtedly made it very difficult for the players to balance their sound. Knowledgeable authorities of the period, such as Allen Dodworth and G.F. Patton,[3] fully recognized the difficulties that would occur with bells pointing in

different directions, and they offered advice to alleviate the problems. Dodworth, for example, recommended using OTS style horns for bands whose purposes are strictly military in nature—"as they throw all the tone [behind] to those who are marching to it"—and upright instruments for all other bands "whose business is not exclusively military."[4] Although Patton states that he is "well-satisfied that 'Over shoulder' horns of every description are more easily blown and have better vibrating qualities than those of any other shape," he seems to prefer the bell front pattern for cornets—"on account of compactness"—and the bell upright pattern for all the larger horns. He goes on to say:

> Whatever pattern of instruments may be selected, it is important that the bells of those used for the accompaniment should point in one direction, so that the sound waves proceeding from the horns by which the Harmony notes are produced may flow together as from a common starting point and blend in a proper and effective manner.

Patton concludes by stating that it makes no difference which way the bells of the cornets point, "since the air [melody] of any piece, being a distinct part, and played upon the most piercing horns, is sufficiently well marked to be heard and recognized."[5]

Patton's preference for bell front and upright instruments is revealing. By 1875, the year that he published his guide to brass band arranging, interest in OTS instruments had waned somewhat; they had served a useful purpose during the Civil War and were no longer in vogue. By the end of the nineteenth century most types of saxhorns were replaced by modern brass instruments as the multicolored (woodwind-brass-percussion) band gradually supplanted the homogeneous sounding cornet-saxhorn brass band.[6]

Because Civil War brass instruments are predominantly conically bored and pitched a perfect fourth higher than modern brass instruments, they produce a

(1) In an article titled "Band Music Then and Now" that appeared in the *American Art Journal*, July 17, 1880, Harvey Dodworth said: " Speaking of instruments, bugles used to be the principal, with trumpets, trombones, serpents and ophicleides. Then my father, Thomas Dodworth, and my elder brother, Allen, invented a very powerful and effective instrument, to which they gave the name ebor corno, and it was identically the same subsequently brought out in France by Saxe [sic], and there christened the saxe-horn. But my father and brother got it up, and we used it in the old National Band, years before the Frenchmen knew anything about it. Our band changed from the bugle to the cornet principle, valves instead of keys in all its instruments, and those made for us to our order were on the principle of the Saxe instruments all the way through, except that the bells of ours were over our shoulders, and threw the sound back, instead of turned upward. Many of those old instruments are in use yet, and hold their own even among the most modern." For a discussion of the question of who designed the first OTS instruments, see William A. Bufkin, *Union Bands of the Civil War* (Ph.D. dissertation, The Louisiana State University, 1973), Chapter V.

(2) Bufkin, pp. 170, 172.

(3) Two important publications that span nearly a quarter of a century, Dodworth's *Brass Band School* (New York: H.B. Dodworth, 1853) and G.F. Patton's *Practical Guide to the Arrangement of Band Music* (New York: John Stratton, 1875), provide a fascinating glimpse of the brass band movement before and after the Civil War.

(4) Dodworth, p. 12.

(5) Patton, p. 43. In a question and answer column in the 1876 Stratton Band Instruments catalogue (p. 10), one reads: "Query No. 11—Our instruments are 'Over-the-shoulder' and 'bell-fronts.' When the band is on parade, should the cornet players march in the front or rear ranks?" Presumably, John Stratton wrote this humorous response: "Put the cornet players in the front rank, and make them march *backward*, so that the sound of all the instruments will go the same way. It may be a little inconvenient for them, but they richly deserve it for being so stupid as to get front cornets to use with over-the-shoulder instruments."

(6) In an interesting article published in the supplement to *Harper's Weekly* dated September 28, 1889, Leon Mead wrote: "At present there are over ten thousand military bands in the United States. In the smaller cities they average twenty-five men each [usually six woodwinds, fifteen brasses, and percussion]. In small country towns they number from twelve to eighteen members."

brilliant but mellow and homogeneous sound from E-flat soprano down to E-flat bass. (The comparatively high range of early brass bands evolved because the first successful chromatic brass instruments were keyed bugles.) The soprano instruments, whether pitched in E-flat or B-flat, sound a great deal mellower than modern trumpets; their tone is similar to the sound of modern cornets and flugelhorns. E-flat alto horns sound like modern alto horns, but quite unlike French horns. B-flat tenor horns, baritones and E-flat basses produce tone qualities that are somewhat like the sound of their modern descendants the euphonium and tuba; however, the sound is paler because the old horns have comparatively smaller bores and the basses are pitched higher than modern tubas. The record sampler included with this book provides a good example of the sound of Civil War era brass instruments. The music was recorded by Heritage Americana Cornet-Saxhorn Brass Band of Washington, D.C., using period instruments.

INSTRUMENTS BY SAMUEL GRAVES

Circular cornet in B-flat. Made by Graves & Co., Boston, early 1860s. German silver with three string rotary valves. Elrod Collection.

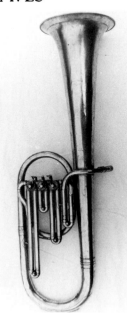

Upright baritone or bass in B-flat. Marked "Gilmore, Graves & Co., Boston," c. 1864-65. German silver with three string rotary valves. Jon Hall Collection. Patrick Gilmore was for a brief time in the mid-1860s in partnership with Samuel Graves. Toward the end of the Civil War, competition was keen among instrument makers, particularly in Boston. The Gilmore-Graves partnership may have resulted from an attempt by Graves to garner additional business through name recognition; Gilmore was a well-known bandleader and cornet vituoso.

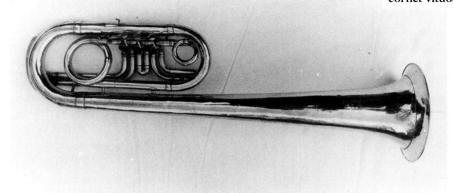

OTS baritone or bass in B-flat. Made by Graves & Co., Boston, c. 1862. German silver with three string rotary valves. Jon Hall Collection.

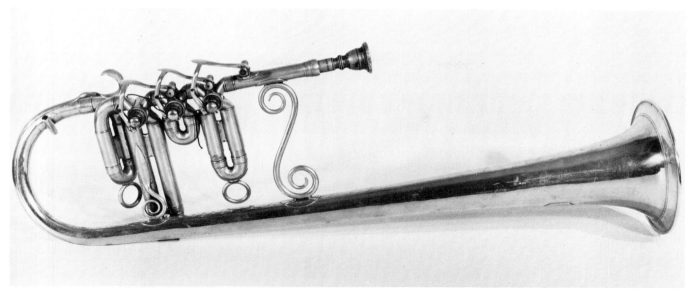

OTS soprano saxhorn in E-flat. Marked "Allen & Hall Makers, Washington St., Boston," c. 1862. German silver with three Allen rotary valves. Elrod Collection.

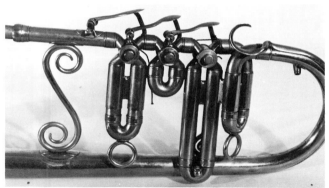

Close up of Allen valves. The design was developed by J. Lathrop Allen of Boston around 1850. The rotors of Allen valves are longer and much smaller in diameter than other rotary valves; therefore, the windways are flattened where the tubing enters the valves. The small diameter rotors operated with exceptional quickness and ease.

Circular cornet in B-flat. Marked "Manufactured by J. Lathrop Allen, No. 17 Harvard Place, Boston," late 1850s. German silver with four Allen rotary valves. Kurt Stein Collection. The fourth valve on this horn, which is played with the left hand, is a descending valve; when engaged it pitches the instrument in A-flat.

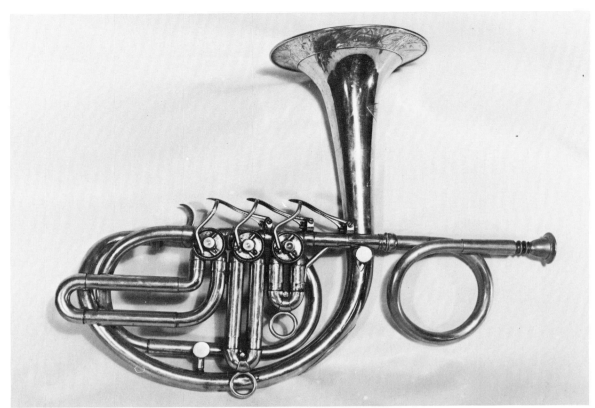

Circular cornet in B-flat. Made by E.G. Wright, Boston, c. 1855. German silver with three string rotary valves. David and Rhoda Lee Burchuk Collection. This dual purpose instrument was originally equipped with two bells and two lead pipes. The circular lead pipe seen here pitches the instrument in A-flat; it can be replaced with a shorter pipe to pitch the instrument in B-flat. The bell on the instrument is detachable; it can be replaced with one that points backward (over the shoulder) for marching use. Note the reverse order of the first and second valve loops. Early valve brass makers often placed the shortest valve loop first. This apparently changed when it was discovered that it was more convenient to place this loop between the other two.

Below: OTS soprano saxhorn in B-flat. Made by E.G. Wright & Co., Boston, early 1860s. German silver with three string rotary valves. Elrod Collection.

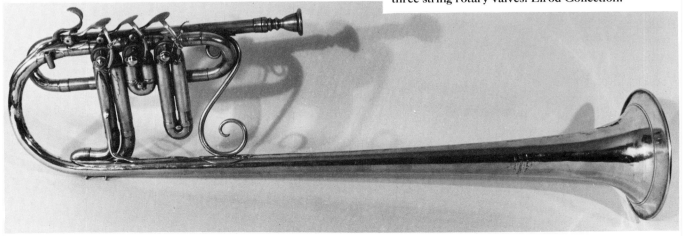

Cornet in B-flat. Made by E.G. Wright, Boston, c. 1865-66. Brass with German silver trim and three string rotary valves. Elrod Collection.

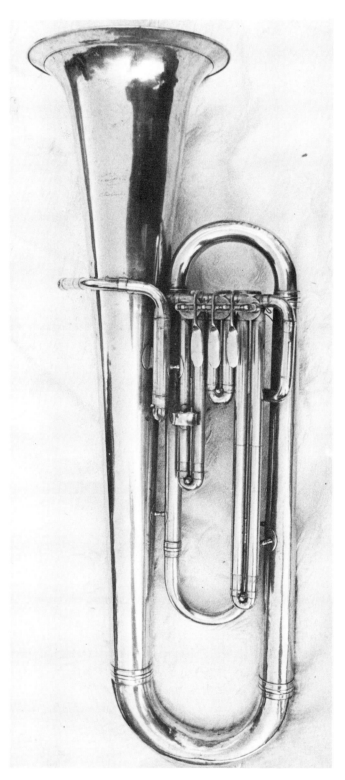

Upright bass in E-flat. Made by E.G. Wright & Co., Boston, c. 1862. German silver with three side action string rotary valves Jon Hall Collection. The inscription "5th Mass. Cavalry" is engraved on the bell under the maker's name.

Circular cornet in B-flat. Marked "Isaac Fiske, Maker, Worcester, Mass.," c. 1855. German silver with five string rotary valves. Elrod Collection. The three valves on the left are the ordinary ones played with the right hand. The other two valves are played with the index and middle fingers of the left hand. The valve on the right is an ascending or cut off valve; it raises the pitch of the instrument one whole step. The valve next to it lowers the pitch two and one-half steps. This versatile yet impractical cornet, which is equipped with two removeable shanks, three adjustable crooks, and two mouthpieces, can be pitched in A-flat, B-flat, C, D, and E-flat. As seen here, the instrument is pitched in E-flat; however, B-flat is the basic key of the instrument.

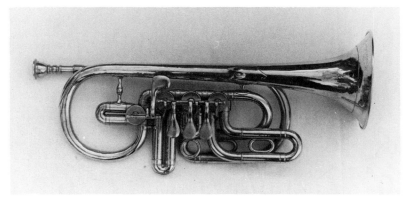

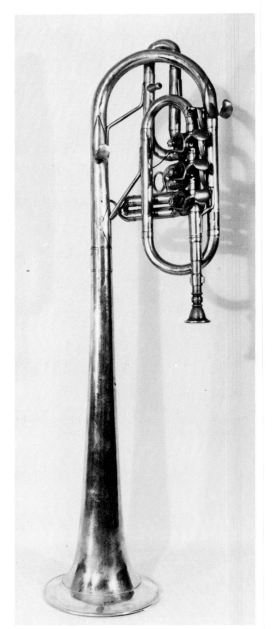

Cornet in B-flat. Made by Isaac Fiske, Worcester, Massachusetts, c. 1862. German silver with four side action string rotary valves. Jon Hall Collection. The upward positioned fourth valve on this instrument is played with the index finger of the left hand.

OTS soprano saxhorn in B-flat. Made by Isaac Fiske, Worcester, Massachusetts, c. 1861. German silver with three string rotary valves. Elrod Collection.

OTS soprano saxhorn in E-flat. Made by John F. Stratton, New York, c. 1865. Brass with three string rotary valves. Elrod Collection. Stratton manufactured instruments which were widely used by Union and Confederate musicians during the war. In 1865 he established a music publishing business and began issuing a music series titled *Stratton's Military Band Journal.*

JOHN F. STRATTON,

MANUFACTURER OF

Brass and German Silver Rotary Valve

MUSICAL INSTRUMENTS,

OF THE

LATEST AND MOST IMPROVED STYLES,

Right: Flugelhorn in E-flat. Made by John F. Stratton, New York, c. 1860s. Brass with three string rotary valves. Elrod Collection. Because the conical bore of this instrument is extremely wide it can be called a valved bugle.

OTS soprano saxhorn in E-flat. Marked "H.B. Dodworth, N.Y.," c. 1863-64. German silver with three string rotary valves. Elrod Collection. This instrument probably was manufactured by John F. Stratton for Harvey Dodworth. The horn belonged to George O. Mead who served with the band of the 144th New York Volunteer Infantry from October 1864 to July 1865.

Cornet in E-flat. Made by C.A. Zoebisch & Sons, New York, c. 1861. Brass with German silver trim and three string rotary valves. Elrod Collection. The coffin-like case is original equipment.

C. A. ZOEBISCH & SONS,
163 WILLIAM STREET,
NEW YORK,
Manufacturers and Importers of all kinds of
MUSICAL INSTRUMENTS

Cornet in B-flat. Made by C.A. Zoebisch & Sons, New York, late 1860s. Brass with three string rotary valves. Elrod Collection.

Cornet in B-flat. Made by C.A. Zoebisch & Sons, New York, c. 1863. German silver with three side action string rotary valves. Elrod Collection.

Above: OTS bass saxhorn in B-flat. Made by Klemm and Brother, Philadelphia, c. 1861. Brass with three mechanical linkage rotary valves. Fred Benkovic Collection. The protective knob and the mechanical linkage valves on this instrument indicate that it probably was made in Europe. American makers and dealers sometimes imported instruments and sold them under their own names.

Incomplete set of OTS saxhorns. Made by Klemm & Brother, Philadelphia, c. 1861. Brass with German silver trim and string rotary valves. Elrod Collection. These instruments appear to be from a matched set; the set may have been used by a band from the Reading, Pennsylvania, area during the Civil War. The instruments are from left to right: E-flat alto, two B-flat tenors, E-flat bass, and, horizontally, B-flat baritone.

OTS soprano saxhorn in E-flat. Made by Martin, Poll-mann & Co., New York, c. 1872. Brass with German silver trim and three string rotary valves. Elrod Collection. The telescopic tuning shank (shown below) is used to adjust the overall pitch of the instrument.

Cornet in E-flat. Made by W. Seefeldt, Philadelphia, c. 1862. German silver with three string rotary valves. Elrod Collection.

Left: Upright soprano saxhorn in E-flat. Made by H. Lehnert, Philadelphia, c. 1867. Brass with three string rotary valves that are modeled after Allen's patented valve design. Elrod Collection. The upright shape is the characteristic style of the saxhorn as originally designed and built by Adolphe Sax in the early 1840s. (However, Sax's prototype instruments had Berliner piston valves, not string rotary valves.)

Cornet in E-flat. Made by E.G. Wright & Co., Boston, c. 1861-62. German silver with three side action string rotary valves. The engraving on the bell reads: "Presented to Oscar F. Clisbee, by the Officers and Privates of Co. G, 24th Regt. Wisconsin Vol. Inf. (1862)." Courtesy of the Constance Wachman family.

OTS ALTO SAXHORNS

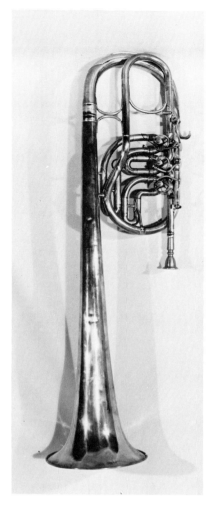

OTS alto horn in E-flat. Marked "Wm. Hall & Son, 543 Broadway, N.Y.," c. 1864. German silver with three string rotary valves. Elrod Collection. The characteristics of this instrument—configuration, shape of the shield, and so on—indicate that it may have been made by John F. Stratton for William Hall, who owned a music store in New York City.

OTS alto horn in E-flat. Marked "W. Seefeldt, Maker, Phila.," c. 1868. Brass with three string rotary valves. Elrod Collection.

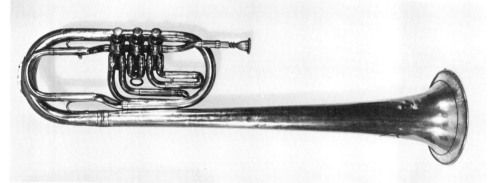

OTS alto horn in E-flat. Marked "Slater & Martin, N.Y.," c. 1868. Brass with three Berliner piston valves. Elrod Collection. The short, stout Berliner "pumpen" valve was common in America from the 1840s through the 1870s because it was durable and inexpensive to make. However, by the end of the nineteenth century, the Berliner valve, along with most other piston valve designs, was supplanted by the Perinet valve.

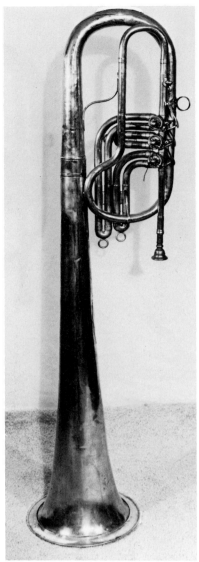

OTS tenor saxhorn in B-flat. Marked "John F. Stratton, 105 & 107 E. 22d St. N.Y.," c. 1864. German silver with three string rotary valves. Elrod Collection.

OTS tenor saxhorn in B-flat. Made by Isaac Fiske, Worcester, Massachusetts, c. 1861. German silver with three string rotary valves. Elrod Collection.

OTS tenor saxhorn in B-flat. Marked "G. Freemantle. MAKER late of Graves & Co: BOSTON.," c. 1862. Brass with three string rotary valves. Formerly Elrod Collection; present owner unknown. George Freemantle worked for Samuel Graves prior to 1862.

Upright baritone or bass in B-flat. Unsigned, possibly made in Philadelphia, c. 1860s. Brass with German silver trim and three string rotary valves (leaf spring design). Elrod Collection.

Upright baritone in B-flat. Made by C.A. Zoebisch & Sons, New York, c. 1862. German silver with three string rotary valves. Elrod Collection.

Upright baritone in B-flat. Made by Hall & Quimby, Boston, c. 1867. Brass with three side action string rotary valves. Elrod Collection.

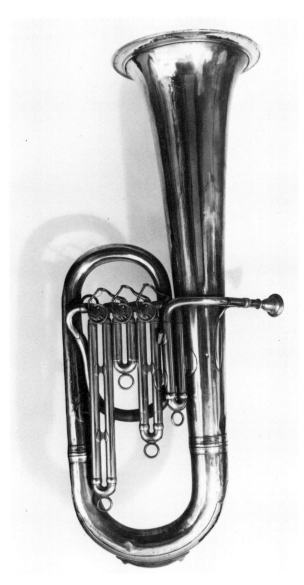

Upright bass in E-flat. Marked "E. Seltmann Maker Phila.," late 1860s. Brass with nickel silver mounts and three string rotary valves. Kurt Stein Collection.

Upright bass saxhorn in E-flat. Made by Slater & Martin, N.Y., c. 1868. Brass with German silver trim and three string rotary valves. Elrod Collection.

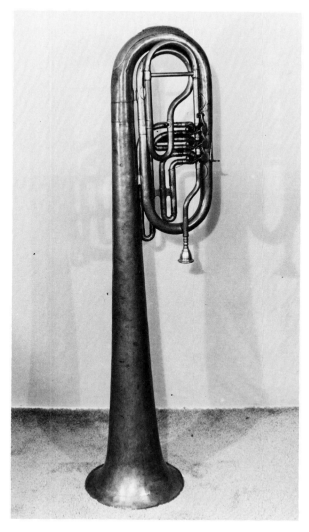

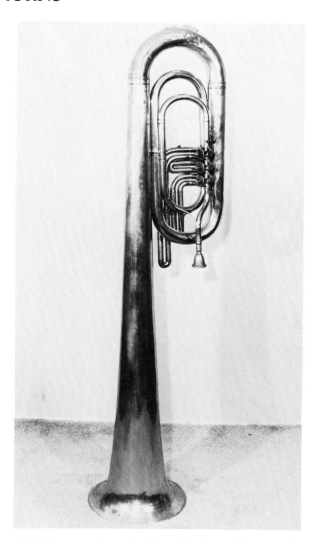

OTS bass saxhorn in E-flat. Made by Kummer & Schet-elich, Baltimore, c. 1864. Brass with three string rotary valves. Elrod Collection.

OTS bass saxhorn in E-flat. Made by Christian R. Stark, New York, c. 1860. German silver with three string rotary valves. Elrod Collection.

Close up of American string linkage rotary valves. String rotary valves and Berliner piston valves were the two most widely used valve designs during the Civil War. Courtesy of Steve Slyvia and Mike O'Donnell.

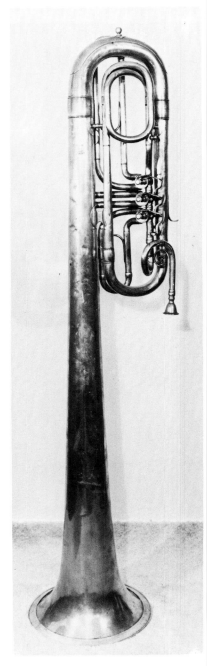

OTS bass saxhorn in E-flat (front and back views). Made by Allen & Hall, Boston, c. 1862. German silver with four Allen rotary valves. Elrod Collection. The fourth valve, which can be seen in the left photo, lowers the instrument to B-flat; it is played with the index finger of the left hand. The flattened or "pinched" windways, which are typical of Allen valves, can be seen where the tubing enters and exits the valves.

OTS bass saxhorn in E-flat. Unsigned, possibly made in Europe, c. 1852. Brass with German silver trim and three internally corked string rotary valves. Elrod Collection. The original mechanical linkage valves on this instrument were converted to string linkage. Note the protective knob on the instrument and the removeable "pigtail" lead pipe.

Bb Cornet, Round.

Bb Cornet—Bell Upright.

Eb Cornet—Bell Front.

S. T. GORDON,

Importer and Dealer in all kinds of

MUSICAL MERCHANDISE,

And Manufacturers of the latest Patterns and most improved Styles of

Brass and German Silver Piston and Rotary Valve Musical Instruments,

706 BROADWAY, N. Y.

Owing to the great demand for our BRASS and GERMAN SILVER Musical Instruments for BANDS, we have been obliged to enlarge our facilities and make extraordinary improvements in our machinery, in order to enable us to supply our customers with the utmost promptness and dispatch. It is our intention to keep full setts of BRASS and GERMAN SILVER Instruments constantly on hand ; also, a large variety of ORCHESTRA CORNETS, both top and side action, bell front, upright and round ; in fact, every SHAPE, STYLE and PATTERN ever made in this or any other country. We would, therefore, invite LEADERS of Bands, individual musicians, and those contemplating forming New Bands, to get our terms before purchasing elsewhere. We fully warrant all instruments manufactured by us, and GUARANTEE PERFECT SATISFACTION. We also allow Bands six days to try these instruments, the express agent retaining the amount of bill; at the end of that time, if not satisfactory, to be carefully repacked and returned to the express agent, and the money refunded. These are great advantages to many living far away from market.

We have also made large additions to our immense stock of FOREIGN GOODS, and our arrangements for obtaining them, through our agent in Europe, give us many advantages. Our stock of STRINGS comprises some of the choicest to be found in the market ; among them we have FRENCH, GERMAN and ITALIAN—the latter ought to be more known to be appreciated. Knowing full well the value of first-class Violin Strings for professional use, we have taken the greatest pains to have them made of the best stock, and by the most experienced workmen, and shipped direct for our trade. Our VIOLINS, GUITARS, VIOLONCELLOS, VIOLIN BOWS, VIOLIN TRIMMINGS, &c., are from the best makers in Europe. Also, our Domestic Department will be found constantly supplied with the best of goods, made expressly to our order. For prices, &c., &c., please refer to our Price List on the following pages.

Bb Cornet—Over the Shoulder.

Bb Bass—Over the Shoulder.

PRICE LIST OF INSTRUMENTS.	Brass Piston Valves.	Brass, with Rotary Valves.	Brass, with G. S. Valves and Trimming.	Ger. Silver Throughout, Rotary Valves.
Eb Cornet	$23.00	$38.00	$45.00	$ 50.00
Bb "	25.00	41.00	48.00	54.00
Eb Alto	32.00	52.00	60.00	66.00
Bb Tenor	36.00	58.00	65.00	72.00
Bb Baritone	40.00	64.00	72.00	80.00
Bb Bass	45.00	69.00	78.00	88.00
Eb Contrabass	50.00	82.00	96.00	110.00
Eb " large	60.00	92.00	110.00	120.00
French Horn, 4 crook		75.00		
" " 6 "		80.00		
Bb Slide Trombone		25.00		
Bb Valve Trombone	36.00	58.00		
Bb Orch. Cornet, 3 valves, top-action		44.00	50.00	57.00
Bb " " 4 "		54.00	62.00	72.00
Bb " " 3 " side-action		49.00	55.00	62.00
Bb " " 4 "		60.00	69.00	77.00
C " " 3 " top-action		45.00	52.00	59.00
C " " 3 " side-action		50.00	55.00	64.00
Echo for Bb Orch. Cornet, 4 valves		10.00	13.00	15.00

Additional Rotary Valves for above Instruments, from $8 to $12 extra.

The Orchestra Cornet in Bb, top-action, may be ordered with an extra Bb Bell over the shoulder. Price for Brass, $7; and for German Silver, $10.

Every description of Brass or German Silver Instruments made to order. The leading styles constantly on hand, and all orders filled at short notice.

In ordering instruments, be particular to state whether you wish the Bell upright, over the shoulder, or circular in shape, and if they are to be used in orchestra or street bands.

Infantry Bugles and Cavalry Trumpets of Brass, Copper or German Silver, all kinds.

Combination of Instruments for Bands.

KIND OF INSTRUMENT.	NUMBER OF PIECES.										
Eb Cornet	2	2	2	2	2	3	3	3	3	4	4
Bb "	1	1	2	2	2	2	2	2	2	2	3
Eb Alto	2	2	2	2	2	2	3	3	3	3	3
Bb Tenor	1	2	2	2	2	2	2	3	3	3	3
Bb Baritone	1	1	1	1	1	1	1	1	1	1	1
Bb Bass				1	1	1	1	1	2	2	2
Eb " Tuba	1	1	1	1	1	1	1	1	1	1	1
Eb " Large					1	1	1	1	1	1	1
Total No. of Instruments	8	9	10	11	12	13	14	15	16	17	18

*** Drums and Cymbals to be added.　　　　**LIBERAL DISCOUNT TO THE TRADE.**

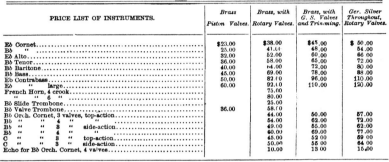

Bb Baritone—Over the Shoulder.

Bb Tenor—Over the Shoulder.

Eb Cornet—Over the Shoulder.

Eb Contrabass—Over the Shoulder.

Bb Cornet—Over the Shoulder.

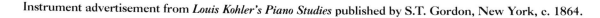

Bb. Orchestra Cornet—Top Action, Long Pattern.

Eb Alto—Over the Shoulder.

Bb. Orchestra Cornet—Side Action, Short Pattern.

Instrument advertisement from *Louis Kohler's Piano Studies* published by S.T. Gordon, New York, c. 1864.

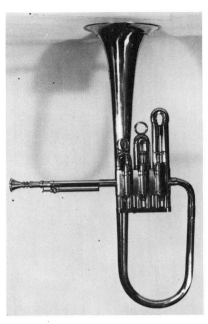

Left: Upright soprano saxhorn in E-flat. Made by Isaac Fiske, Worcester, Mass., c. 1848. Brass with three Vienna twin-piston valves and case with sliding door. Fred Benkovic Collection.

Right: Cornet in E-flat. Made by C.H. Eisenbrandt, Baltimore. Silver with gold plated brass trim and three side action rotary valves designed by the maker. Fred Benkovic Collection. The inscription on the bell reads: "C.H. Eisenbrandt Patent Valves and Patent Slide. July 4th, 1854 January 21st, 1858. Baltimore."

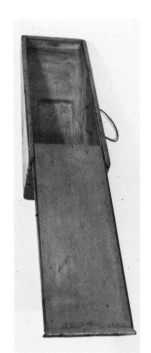

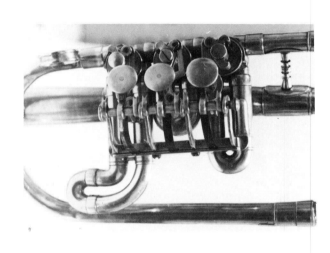

Circular cornet in E-flat. Made by Isaac Fiske, Worcester, Mass., c. 1860. German silver with three string rotary valves. Fred Benkovic Collection.

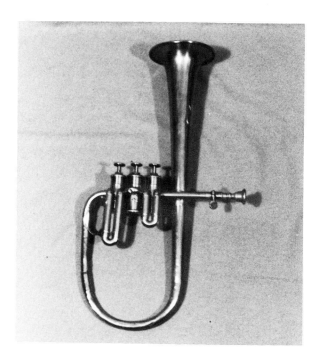

Upright soprano saxhorn in E-flat. Made by Daniel Hess, New York, in 1864. Brass with three Berliner piston valves. An important advantage to this shape is that it permits the tube leading from the mouthpiece to reach the valves very quickly, so that upon leaving the valves the main tube may begin its gradual, conical expansion to the bell. The primary factor contributing to the characteristic mellow sound of the saxhorn is the conical expansion of the tubing. Fred Benkovic Collection.

Upright alto horn in E-flat. Made by Gilmore & Co., Boston, c. 1865. Brass with three side action string rotary valves. Fred Benkovic Collection. Patrick Gilmore, the famous bandleader, was in the instrument manufacturing business for a few years in the mid-1860s.

Upright alto horn in E-flat. Made by C.A. Zoebisch & Sons, New York, early 1860s. German silver with three string rotary valves. Fred Benkovic Collection.

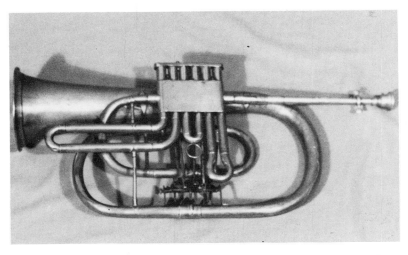

Bell front alto horn in E-flat. Marked "F.G. Kaiser, Cincinnati, Ohio," c. 1856. Brass with three Vienna twin-piston valves. Fred Benkovic Collection. This unusual instrument, which is shaped like a cornet, can be pitched in the key of F by inserting a shorter lead pipe.

Right: Upright baritone or bass in B-flat. Made by E.G. Wright, Boston, c. 1861-62. German silver with four side action string rotary valves. Fred Benkovic Collection. The inscription on the bell reads: "Presented to Daniel Davis by the non-commissioned officers and privates of Co. I, 24th Wisc. V.I."

OTS bass saxhorn in B-flat. Made by D.C. Hall, Boston, c. 1862. German silver with three string rotary valves. Fred Benkovic Collection. This instrument was played by Joseph L. Smith of the 1st Brigade Band, 3rd Division, 15th Army Corps.

Upright bass in E-flat. Marked with the name W.C. Peters, Cincinnati, c. 1860. German silver with three string rotary valves. Fred Benkovic Collection. William C. Peters was not an instrument manufacturer; he was an instrument dealer and music publisher. In 1859 he published a popular brass band collection titled *Peters' Sax Horn Journal.*

Cornet in E-flat. Made by C.A. Zoebisch & Sons, New York, c. 1860. Brass with three side action string rotary valves. This extremely wide bore instrument was played by Will N. Butner of the 33rd North Carolina Regiment Band. The other instruments on this page are thought to have been used by the same band. Courtesy Old Salem Restoration, Winston-Salem, N.C.

Right: Upright bass saxhorn in E-flat. Unsigned, c. 1860. Brass with three Berliner piston valves. Courtesy Old Salem Restoration, Winston-Salem, N.C.

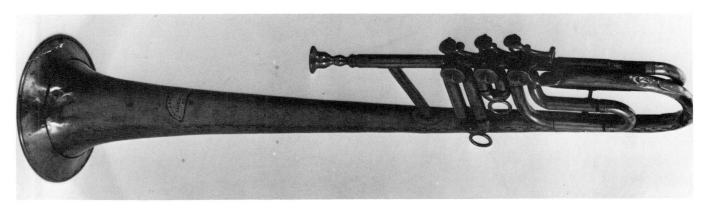

OTS soprano saxhorn in B-flat. Made by Kummer & Schetelich, Baltimore, c. 1865. Brass with three string rotary valves. Courtesy Old Salem Restoration, Winston-Salem, N.C.

WOODWINDS

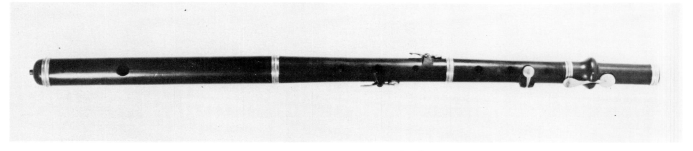

Flute in C. Made by William Hall & Son, N.Y., c. 1850s. Rosewood with four silver keys in wood saddle mounts. Jack Silver Collection.

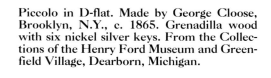

Piccolo in D-flat. Made by George Cloose, Brooklyn, N.Y., c. 1865. Grenadilla wood with six nickel silver keys. From the Collections of the Henry Ford Museum and Greenfield Village, Dearborn, Michigan.

Left: Clarinet in E-flat. Made by Martin & Son, Paris, c. 1860s. Rosewood with 12 nickel silver keys and two rings. Jack Silver Collection.

Right: Clarinet in B-flat. Made by Joseph Wallis, London, late 1860s. Rosewood with 12 nickel silver keys and two rings. Jack Silver Collection.

Woodwind instruments similar to those pictured here were sometimes used by Civil War era brass bands.

TRUMPETS

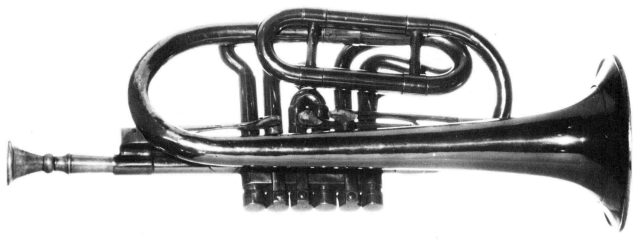

Trumpet in E-flat. Made by Graves & Co., Winchester, N.H., c. 1840s. Brass with three Vienna twin-piston valves. Robert Rosenbaum Collection. This photo looks upside down, but the instrument is in normal playing position; the leaf-spring valve levers appear just above the main tube.

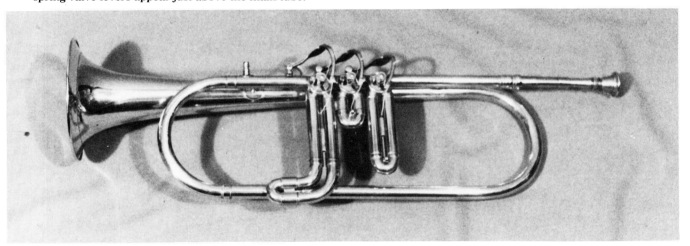

Trumpet in B-flat. Made by Granville Draper, Boston, c. 1860. German silver with three string valves. Fred Benkovic Collection. Although trumpets were sometimes used in brass bands, the preferred instruments were the cornet and soprano saxhorn.

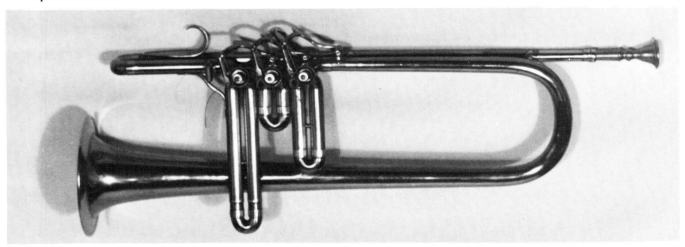

Trumpet in B-flat. Made by B.F. Richardson, Boston, c. 1861. Brass with three string rotary valves. Fred Benkovic Collection. The configuration of this trumpet is unusual in that the bell is positioned at the bottom of the instrument.

Tenor trombone in B-flat. Unsigned, possibly made in Europe, c. 1830s. Brass with reinforced bell. Elrod Collection.

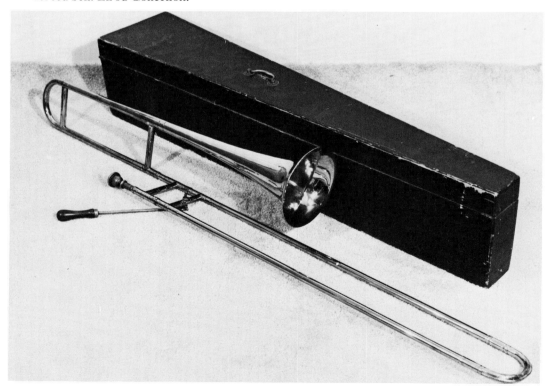

Bass trombone in G. Unsigned, possibly made in America between 1835-45. Brass with slide extension handle. Elrod Collection. Slide trombones such as those seen here were used in early brass bands; however, they were relatively uncommon during the Civil War. (Tenor saxhorns were used.)

VALVE TROMBONES

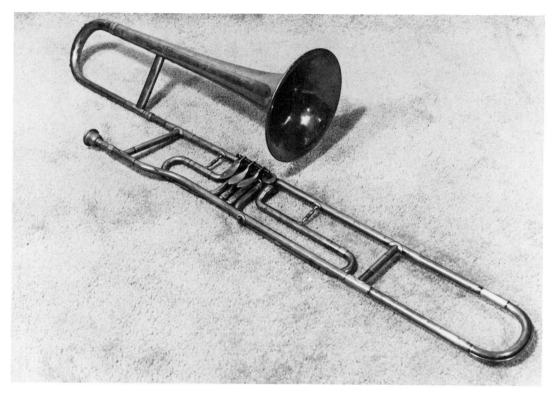

Valve trombone in B-flat. Unsigned, possibly made in New York, c. 1860s. Brass with German silver trim and three side action string rotary valves. Elrod Collection.

Valve trombone in B-flat. Marked "Made by Boston Instrument Manufy.," c. 1869. Brass with three side action string rotary valves. Garofalo Collection. Valve trombones such as those seen here were fairly common in brass bands after the Civil War.

Christopher Spencer, c. 1855. This young musician was a member of Colt's Armory Band of Hartford Connecticut. His OTS soprano saxhorn probably was made by Samuel Graves. Courtesy of Honiss Collection and Nancy Savin.

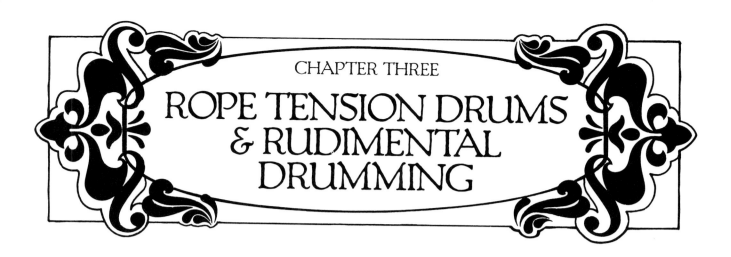

CHAPTER THREE

ROPE TENSION DRUMS & RUDIMENTAL DRUMMING

An interesting yet somewhat neglected aspect of brass band instruments and music is that of rope tension drums and rudimental drumming. When researching material for this chapter, we were surprised to find that very little had been written about the instruments, equipment and performance practices of Civil War era drummers. Fortunately, what is lacking in print is more than made up for in the knowledge and artistry of a few talented musicians such as George and Cathy Carroll of Washington, D.C., who not only have studied the subject in great detail, but also have mastered the skills of nineteenth century rudimental drumming on period instruments. Much of the information that follows was graciously provided by Mr. Carroll.

FIELD MUSICIAN DRUMMERS

Most Civil War drummers were field musicians not associated with military bands. Infantry companies had drummers and fifers, but only large units (regiments and brigades) had bands. Familiarity with the techniques and equipment of field musician drummers is essential for an understanding of the performance practices of military band drummers because both types appear to have used the same rudimental style and their instruments were similar.

Union and Confederate army regulations authorized each infantry company to have two field musicians, usually a drummer and a fifer. Company drummers and fifers (who were humorously called "sheepskin fiddlers" and "straw-blowers") were used to form regimental drum corps. A regiment at full strength could provide a drum corps of 10 drummers and 10 fifers under the leadership of a drum major (a non-commissioned officer).

Every daily activity of the infantry soldier was controlled by the company or regimental drums and fifes. A day's routine usually included the playing of some fifty short pieces to initiate, accompany, or end military activities. Field maneuvers were controlled by the same means.

Given the responsibilities entrusted to field musicians, most of whom were young boys ages 12 to 16, it is not surprising to find that their training was rigorous. Federal drummers who enlisted in the Regular Army were trained at two military music facilities ("Schools for Practice") at Governor's Island (in New York Harbor) and Newport Barracks (Kentucky). Manuals such as Bruce and Emmett's *The Drummers' and Fifers' Guide*[1] were used to instruct drummers in the techniques of rudimental drumming. Bruce and Emmett's manual contains notated drum rudiments based on a tradition of drum playing which had been passed down by rote.

Rudiments are fundamental ways of making sounds on a drum. In *The Drummers' and Fifers' Guide*, the long roll comes first, followed by eight different types of rolls and more than two dozen additional rudiments which provide a wide variety of effects to embellish the drum stokes that sound basic rhythm patterns. (The guide also contains a large collection of music for field use with the drum parts elaborated with fully notated rudiments.) While Bruce and Emmett employ 36 rudiments in their manual, over 100 rudiments are known to have been used during the Civil War.

The tradition of learning to play the drum by rote rather than by note was still very much alive during the Civil War. Some drummers of volunteer militia units learned their craft in this manner, and they learned it "on-the-job." Militia drummers were often taught by a drum major who had been trained at one of the Schools for Practice or by an experienced drummer who happened to be in their ranks. The rote

---

(1) Published by Firth, Pond & Co., New York, 1861, 1862, and 1865. According to George Carroll, *The Drummers' and Fifers' Guide* is an historic milestone in the art of fifing and drumming, and one of the most important books of its type ever published.

method worked reasonably well because all field musicians were required to perform the "camp duty" music from memory.

DRUM MANUFACTURING

Drum making was an established trade industry in this country before the Civil War. The conflict, of course, greatly stimulated the enterprise by creating an enormous demand for percussion instruments. U.S. Army records show that over 32,000 drums were purchased between 1861 and 1865.[2] With the potential for profits so great, many individuals and companies became directly or indirectly involved in the making, distribution, and selling of drums during the war.[3]

As was the situation with brass instrument manufacturing, the important centers of drum making were located in the industrialized Northeast. Boston, New York, and Philadelphia were the most active centers of trade in this regard, with Philadelphia having three companies whose labels frequently appear on extant drums of the period—C. & F. Soistmann, Ernst Vogt, and Horstmann Brothers.

It should be noted that government contracts usually did not specify exact dimensions or designs for drums. Eagle emblazonments were common on drums, but the eagle designs varied. A regulation describing a U.S. Army drum did exist; however, it apparently was only used as a guide.[4]

The typical drum section of a Civil War brass band consisted of three instruments—rope tension snare (side) drum, bass drum, and a pair of cymbals.[5] A few large bands of the period used more than one snare drum, but that was atypical.

The design and construction of nineteenth century rope tension drums were based on established patterns and methods of drum making that were more than three centuries old. In general, a cylinder-shaped wooden shell was used, with "heads" made of animal skin stretched over the open ends. The edges of the skin heads were soaked and then lapped (tucked) around circular "flesh hoops." These hoops were held in place at the ends of the drum by wooden "counter hoops." Tension on the counter hoops, which influenced the tension of the heads, was controlled by a rope laced through holes drilled in the hoops or fed through cast iron hooks which bore on the hoops.

(2) Cited in Bufkin, *Union Bands of the Civil War*, p. 165. As a general rule, the Federal and Confederate governments did not purchase instruments for bands. Bandsmen either brought their own instruments with them when they joined the army, or they played on new instruments purchased with funds provided by civic groups or by regimental officers and enlisted men.

(3) Bufkin, p. 187, lists nearly three dozen drum makers, dealers and importers who were in business between 1830 and 1865.

(4) Army guidelines state that military drums were to be painted with the arms of the United States on a blue field for the infantry and on a red field for the artillery; the letter of the company and the number of the regiment were to appear under the arms or in a scroll.

(5) In the nineteenth century the snare drum was variously named side drum, small drum or tenor drum. The nomenclature "side drum" was derived from the manner in which the instrument was originally carried—high on the left side. The side drum was an established part of military equipment of European armies as early as the fifteenth century.

Drum section of Captain Rush's brass band. From a composite photograph, early 1860s. The cymbal player is identified on the backmark as Theodore Fowler; the names of the drummers are illegible. Authors' collection.

Leather braces or "ears," each one surrounding two adjoining ropes, were used to adjust the head tension.

The shells of rope tension drums were made of ash, rosewood, maple, white holly, or similar types of pliable wood. Although double and even triple veneered wood was common during the period, cheaply made drums with imitation veneers were sold. It was also possible to purchase custom made drums with fancy inlaid patterns or with richly painted designs.

The top head on the snare drum was called the "batter head" (the beating or playing head); the bottom was the "snare head." Several strands of catgut or rawhide were stretched closely together across the center of the bottom head. These strands, which usually numbered from four to six, were called snares.[6] To control their tension, snares were either placed between the bottom flesh and counter hoops, or they were connected to a "snare strainer" (an adjustable fastener) at one end and a fixed leather attachment or "butt" at the other end. The snares created the unique timbre of the instrument.

The heads of rope tension drums were made of calfskin or sheepskin. The timbre of the snare drum sound was influenced somewhat by the thickness of the skin heads and snares and by the match of the snare head to the batter head. However, the really critical factors influencing the sound were the amount and equal distribution of tension on the heads, the cut of the snare bed in the shell, and the precise placement and tension of the snares. Although a properly adjusted drum could be very crisp and taut, the least amount of dampness changed the tension of the heads, and it didn't take much humidity to make the drum very deep and soggy sounding. Some of the dampness could be compensated for by extra "overhauling," tensioning, but if the humidity was great, the drum continued to deepen in pitch and get sloppier in response.

The dimensions of rope tension drums vary considerably. It is not uncommon today to find period snare drums bearing the same maker's label which have different diameter and depth measurements. Evidently, no effort was expended on mass producing standard sizes, there being no necessity to maintain replacement flesh hoops, heads or snares other than those sufficiently large enough to be trimmed to fit the item replaced. In general, the snare drum shells were about 15 to 16 inches in diameter and 10 to 12 inches in depth, not including the counter hoops.

Bass drums also varied greatly in size, although the large "barrel drums" were common during the period. Give or take a few inches, the widths of bass drums averaged about two feet, with the diameters varying

from under two feet to as much as three feet.

A number of period drums in existence today show evidence of the shells having been reduced in size, that is "cut down." Frequently, the eagle emblazonment is cut off at the top and bottom on snare drums and at the sides on bass drums. The radical alteration of an old drum in this manner probably resulted from an attempt by its owner to produce a brighter, crisper tone with less volume for band application as distinct from field music usage where volume was needed. Because rope tension drums were very light in weight, the reductions in size could not have had much of an effect on the weight to matter. Neither were the military issue snare drums so deep in size to make them impractical for even the youngest, shortest drummer.

Although the overwhelming majority of Civil War drummers played on rope tension drums made of wood, metal shelled drums with rope tension were not uncommon during the war. There are early photographs which depict entire military drum corps using rope tension snare drums with metal shells. Several drums of this type have survived and are in private and public collections. Evidently, metal drums were issued by some regiments. Metal drums were made of brass or German silver, with the latter being slightly more expensive. A number of "presentation" drums with silver shells were also made during the period.

(6) In the introduction to the 1862 edition of *The Drummers' and Fifers' Guide*, George B. Bruce wrote: "In regard to snares, some performers prefer cat-gut, others raw-hide, both are good, but for general use, the raw-hide is preferable, as in wet weather, the cat-gut is the most easily affected by the dampness, which causes a contraction, and prevents the proper vibration."

Rope tension side drum, bass drum, and beater. Side drum made by C. & F. Soistmann, Philadelphia, c. 1858. Bass drum made by William Boucher, Baltimore, c. 1845. Elrod Collection.

Rod tension drums were extremely rare during the Civil War. (The rod tension mechanism was first introduced in Europe in the early 1830s.) We have seen only one photograph of a military band in which the bass drummer is using a narrow, rod tension bass drum that appears to be foreign made. The photograph was not included in the book because it was badly faded. Rod tension drums begin to appear with increasing frequency in band photographs from the 1870s on.

STICKS AND BEATERS

Most period snare drum sticks were made of dark wood such as rosewood, ebony, or cocobolo. Generally they were thick, long, and heavy. (Occasionally, however, a light weight pair of "concert" size sticks reported as dating from the period is found.) Unlike modern snare drum sticks, the old sticks were tapered all the way from the butt end to the tip or playing end. Sometimes a metal cap covered the butt end, but this design was more common on foreign made sticks. Although most early drum sticks were turned entirely from pieces of wood, some were crafted with tips or "beads" made of bone, ivory, or metal. The old sticks, regardless of the material, lend themselves nicely to the open style of drumming that was used in the nineteenth century.

The open drum style demands great skill to execute. Large forearm motions are needed to initiate and sustain vibrations of the skin heads, and the opposite grip sticking technique is required.[7] When applied in performance, the open style of drumming produces a lively sound that is quite different from the closed style used today. Also, modern snare drums produce a lighter, crisper sound because they usually are smaller and have plastic heads and metal snares. The old drums generally have a deep, resonant sound that carries very well out of doors; they produce a distinctive timbre that is unobtainable on modern drums.

Period bass drum beaters came in different sizes ranging from small to large. Some were made of solid wood such as maple or walnut, others had leather or buckskin covered heads (rubber heads came into use in the mid-1870s).[8] Despite published statements to the contrary, covered cotton balls were not used on the heads of bass drum sticks.[9] The material would not have been sufficiently heavy to produce a characteristic sound on a period drum.

The techniques and equipment used to play the rope tension bass drums were more complex than is generally realized today. In addition to using the single beating technique, the player could use the two-stick rudimental bass drumming method, or an alternate style using a heavy, leather covered stick in the right hand for the main beats in the measure and a lighter, "tenor" stick in the left hand for filling in between the main beats.

CRASH CYMBALS

Contrary to opinion held by historians in the 1960s, we now know that cymbals were widely used in military bands during the Civil War. Examination of photographs, muster roles and other primary source material reveals that more often than not cymbals are evident. Civil War bands used cymbals whenever and

(7) With the opposite grip, the left stick was held differently from the right stick. Today, most snare drummers use the matched grip in which both sticks are held the same way.

(8) Bass drum sticks with maple handles and rubber heads were advertised in the John F. Stratton band instrument catalogue in 1876.

(9) Kenneth Olson erroneously states in *Music and Musket* (p. 260) that "bass drum sticks had heavy wooden shafts topped with leather covered cotton balls.'

Inexpensive brass cymbals with leather thong handles. Manufacturer and date unknown. Diameter 12". These cymbals reportedly were used by a musician who served with a Massachusetts regiment during the Civil War. Courtesy Fort Ward Museum, Alexandria, Virginia.

wherever the instrument and player could be found. Our experiences in recreating the music of the Civil War on period instruments have shown that cymbals add much color to the sound of a brass band, especially when heard in the open air.

The cymbals depicted in period photographs of brass bands appear to be somewhat smaller than most modern cymbals. Advertisements in instrument catalogues, such as those published annually in the 1860s and 1870s by the John F. Stratton Company, indicate that cymbals varied in size from around 12 to 14 inches, usually in increments of a half inch.

Although only a relatively few pairs of poor quality, brass cymbals (reputedly old enough to qualify as Civil War era vintage) have survived, good quality Turkish cymbals were imported and sold by music houses in this country well before the Civil War. (The famous Zildjian formula for making Turkish cymbals is over 300 years old.) Some early brass bands undoubtedly purchased and used the more expensive imported cymbals.

The technique of cymbal playing used by Civil War bandsmen presumably was similar to the method used today. The player held the instrument in his hands by grasping wooden handles or leather thongs bolted to the cymbals. The cymbals were crashed

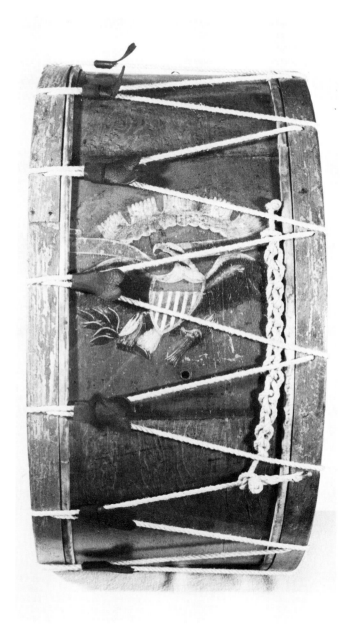

"Allie Turner Drum." Maker's label reads: "Union Manufacturing Company, 184 West Baltimore Street, Baltimore, Maryland, Francis Sauer & Co.," early 1860s. Courtesy William Penn Memorial Museum, Harrisburg, Pa. This drum reputedly was played by Allie Turner, one of the youngest drummerboys in Grant's army. Note in the photo of this unrestored drum that the rope is fed through iron hooks instead of being laced through holes in the hoops.

Cut down bass drum. Made by "Stratton & Foote, No. 31 Maiden Lane, N.Y.," c. 1860s. Courtesy William Penn Memorial Museum, Harrisburg, Pa. This bass drum belonged to Jacob Henderson, a member of the Columbia (Pa.) Cornet Band. Although Henderson is known to have served in the Civil War, it has not been established whether the Columbia Band served as a unit in the war.

together using an off center sliding action to initiate sound vibrations. When employed in marching music, cymbals were used to beat time along with the bass drum.

The occasional appearance of an upturned cymbal attached to a bass drum in period photographs of brass bands indicates that the practice of using one player to cover both bass drum and cymbals was used. How this practice got started is unknown. Practical rather than musical considerations probably caused it to occur.[10]

The exciting, martial sounds of a rope tension drum section performing with a reconstituted Civil War brass band can be heard on the record sampler. Authentic drums are used, played with traditional rudimental techniques.[11]

(10) For more information on the use of bass drum and cymbals in brass bands, see Garofalo & Elrod "Reflections on the Performance Practices of Mid-Nineteenth Century Brass Bands," *Journal of Band Research*, Fall 1981.
(11) The performers are George and Cathy Carroll and Terry Heilman.

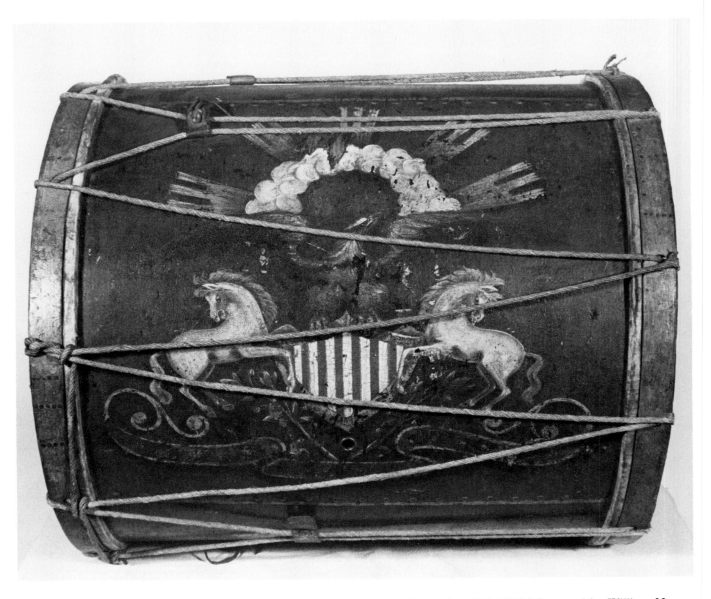

Logan Guards bass drum. Marked "William Keefer, Harrisburg, Penna Oct 15th 1834." Restored by William H. Reamer. Courtesy William Penn Memorial Museum, Harrisburg, Pa. This early barrel drum was first used by a militia unit whose name was once lettered in a scroll below the state seal which forms the drum's decoration. In April of 1861, the drum accompanied the Logan Guards to Washington. The Logan Guards of Lewistown, Pennsylvania, were one of the first units summoned to defend the capital against a feared Confederate attack. An account of the unit's excursion to Washington is written in pencil on one of the drum's heads.

Bass drum with military scene on the shell. Made by John Grosh, East Hempfield Township, Pa., in 1828. Restored by William H. Reamer. Courtesy William Penn Memorial Museum, Harrisburg, Pa. This drum was played by Martin Brubaker, a musician in the Rapho Band of Lancaster County, Pennsylvania, in 1830. Additional inscriptions on the drum indicate that it also may have been used by Kelly's Cornet Band of Elizabethtown during the 1850s, and by the Serandandling Rifles during the Civil War. The drum's decoration depicts a mounted militiaman with sword drawn; a row of tents is seen in the background.

The same bass drum before restoration. An inscription inside the drum says that the instrument was made by a cooper. The drum is constructed like a barrel, except that the support hoops are inside (not outside) the shell.

Augustus Kyle with his drum during the Civil War. A handwritten label pasted to the interior of this drum contains a history of its use by Kyle, who first enlisted with the "Fighting 130th Regiment Pa Vols Infantry" and later served with the 187th Regiment. The history was written at the time of a reunion of the 130th Regiment in 1903. Courtesy William Penn Memorial Museum, Harrisburg, Pa.

Shell of the Kyle drum before restoration.

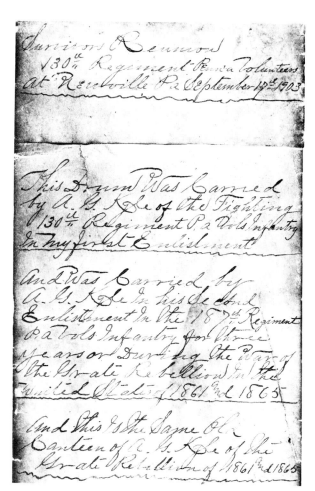

Maker's inscription on the interior of the Kyle drum reads: "Wm. S. Thompkins & Sons Makers Yonkers, N.Y. Drums of all sizes made to order April 1st, 1863."

Handwritten note from the interior of the Kyle drum which documents its use.

"Survivors' Reunion, 130th Regiment Penna Volunteers at Newville, Pa., September 17th, 1903." Kyle is pictured on the right with his drum.

Eagle drum used by Peter Frederick Rothermel as a model for his painting of the Battle of Gettysburg. Manufactured by Horstmann Brothers, Philadelphia, early 1860s. Restored by William H. Reamer. Courtesy William Penn Memorial Museum, Harrisburg, Pa. When Rothermel's daughter donated this drum to the museum, she included an historical note stating that the drum had been found at Gettysburg and that it was used by her father as a model for this 1870 oil painting. The unique feature of the instrument is the bullet hole in the top head. When the drum was restored to playing condition, a plastic patch was used to save the original head.

Manufacturer's label from the interior of the Gettysburg drum.

Detail of Rothermel's painting depicting the drum in the lower center.

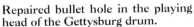

Repaired bullet hole in the playing head of the Gettysburg drum.

WM. H. HORSTMANN & SONS,
No. 51 North Third Street, Philadelphia,

MANUFACTURERS AND IMPORTERS OF

MILITARY GOODS, COACH LACES, AND FRINGES,

Epaulettes, Swords, Sashes, Buttons, Laces, Chapeaux, Pistols, Holsters, Saddle-Cloths, Banners, Flags, Embroideries, &c., &c.
Volunteer Companies and Officers of the Army and Navy, supplied with every article in the Military Line.

LADIES FANCY TRIMMINGS,

Cords, Tassels, Fringes, Buttons, Gimps, Bindings, Braids, &c.

MILITARY CLOTHS AND CASSIMERES.

Horstmann & Sons advertisement which appeared in an 1852 city guide to Philadelphia. The Horstmann family business was established before 1820 by William H. Horstmann, a German immigrant and weaver by trade. In 1842 Horstmann's two sons, William and Sigmund, became partners in the business which was then located at No. 51 North Third Street. After William Sr. retired in 1845, the business continued to prosper under the management of his sons. By 1852 the firm had grown to the point where it was necessary to erect a large manufacturing building at Fifth and Cherry Streets. In the 1860s, Horstmann Brothers had two separate manufacturing units in operation—one for "Dress Trimmings & Carriage Lace," and the other for "Military & Society Goods." Courtesy of Kurt Stein.

Top: Revolutionary War drum. Maker and date unknown. Decoration on drum "Relic of 1776" painted c. 1840. Restored and owned by Fred Benkovic. Period sticks and sling added. This drum reportedly was used by a patriot at Bunker Hill during the American Revolution, by a Vermont drummer during the War of 1812, for recruiting during the Mexican War, and, finally, by a 9th Vermont infantry drummer during the Civil War.

Bottom Left: Snare drum with tack design and period sticks. Drum made by Benjamin & Ely Brown, Connecticut, possibly as early as the 1820s. The tack design has eight diamond shapes surrounding a double circle. Note the large beads and metal caps on the sticks. Courtesy U.S. Marine Corps Museum, Washington, D.C.

Bottom Right: Snare drum with allegorical decoration and identification "York Washington Artillery" (a Pennsylvania unit). Maker and date unknown, possibly dates back to the American Revolution. Fred Benkovic Collection. During the War of 1812 this drum was captured by the British, recaptured by the Americans, and eventually ended up in Fort McHenry, Baltimore. It is not known if the instrument was used during the Civil War.

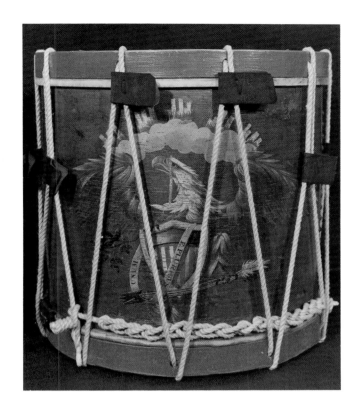

Left: Early nineteenth century eagle drum. Marked "Made by Thomas Bringhurst, Germantown, Philadelphia County, Pa.," c. 1820. Courtesy Cape May County (N.J.) Historical and Genealogical Society.

Right: Pennsylvania militia drum with state seal and motto. Made by William Ent, Germantown, Pa., between 1820-1844. J. Craig Nannos Collection.

Federal artillery drum. Made by Elias Howe, Boston, 1860. Fred Benkovic Collection. Drums with eagle emblazonments painted on a red field signify artillery; those painted on a blue field signify infantry. The 13 stars appearing above the eagle on this drum represent the United States. Photo courtesy of George Carroll.

Snare drum with early eagle design. Maker and date unknown. Fred Benkovic Collection. This beautifully painted eagle drum was used by Joshua Brown during Dorr's Rebellion of 1842. Photo courtesy of George Carroll.

Front and side views of an infantry eagle drum. Maker unknown, c. 1861. The gut snares appearing in the foreground in the left photograph were originally part of the instrument. Tack designs, such as the one seen on the right, were functional as well as decorative. The tacks reinforced the overlapping portion of the shell where the drum was glued together. Photos courtesy of George Carroll.

Confederate eagle drum used by J.L. Nelson, Co. D, unknown regiment. No maker's label, c. 1861. Restored by Fred Benkovic. Courtesy Milwaukee Public Museum. Eleven gold stars representing the Confederate States surround the eagle's head and also appear on the shield. The red and white banner reads: "Confederate States of America." This emblazonment adapts a U.S. eagle design for Confederate usage. Confederate eagle drums are extremely rare.

Eagle drum with five stars. Manufactured by Wm. Boucher, Jr., Baltimore, c. 1861. Restored and owned by Fred Benkovic. This drum, which has five stars painted on the shield and above the eagle, was used by a drummer of the 5th Regiment Maryland National Guard during the Civil War.

Military eagle drum with period sticks and sling. Marked "Manufactured by Horstmann, Brothers & Co., Fifth & Cherry Streets, Philadelphia," c. 1863. The heads, rope, leather braces, and snares are original to the drum. Fred Benkovic Collection.

Back side of a 17th Michigan Infantry drum with Civil War battle honors. Manufactured by Ernst Vogt, Philadelphia, c. 1861. Restored by Fred Benkovic. From the Collections of the Henry Ford Museum and Greenfield Village, Dearborn, Michigan.

Civil War eagle drum. Marked "Ernst Vogt, Phila. Pa., contract Dec. 29, 1864." J. Craig Nannos Collection.

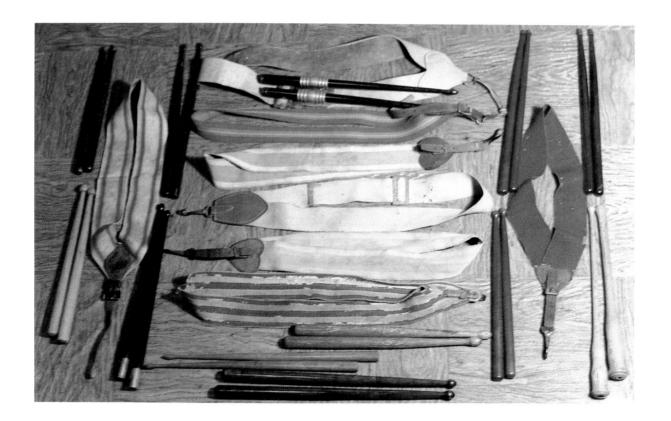

Equipment used by Civil War era snare drummers. The slings are made of cloth webbing (plain or fancy colors) or patent leather. The sticks are made of different types of wood; two of the pairs have brass ornamentation. Courtesy of Fred Benkovic.

Equipment used by Civil War era bass drummers. The slings were made of fine cloth webbing or black leather. The bass drum beaters are made of wood; some have buckskin covered heads. Courtesy of Fred Benkovic.

Top: Ordinary snare drum. Maker unknown, c. 1861. Fred Benkovic Collection. This inexpensive drum with imitation wood grain painted on the shell was used by George Emerson, Co. B, 7th New Hampshire Volunteer Infantry.

Ebony snare drum sticks with ivory tips and caps. Courtesy of Terry Heilman.

Turkish cymbals with original leather carrying case. Manufacturer unknown, c. 1850s. Brass with wooden handles bolted to the cymbals. Diameter 12". Fred Benkovic Collection.

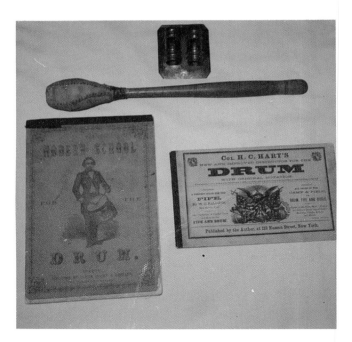

Drum methods such as *Col. H.C. Hart's New and Improved Instructor for the Drum* (right), published in 1862, were used to teach Civil War drummers the craft of rudimental drumming. Although stick holders made of brass (top center) were issued during the war, many drummers preferred to carry their sticks under their belts. Courtesy of Terry Heilman.

CHAPTER FOUR

MILITARY BANDS & BANDSMEN (1861-65)

By 1861 most towns and cities in America had one or more brass bands playing year round both in and out of doors. Bands participated in parades, performed at picnics and dances, and played for political rallies. Many town bands were attached to local militia units. As militia bandsmen, the musicians wore the uniforms of their units. Militia bands periodically participated in musters and other military and patriotic ceremonies. Bands were highly valued by their militia units because they were extremely useful in helping to recruit citizen soldiers.

When the nation rose up in arms after the opening gun at Fort Sumter in April of 1861, bands were in the forefront. Appeals to patriotism were greatly enhanced by the martial strains of military band music. With flags waving and brass bands playing, thousands of eager volunteers were recruited to serve in the newly organized armies. The Civil War had ushered in a new era for brass bands, one that was not matched in any period of American history.

FEDERAL ARMY BANDS

The period from April 1861 to August 1862 could be referred to as the "regimental band period" of the Federal Army. It was a time when hundreds of bands and thousands of bandsmen were mustered in with volunteer regiments and paid solely to furnish military music. Considered noncombatants, these regimental bandsmen generally were not required to perform duties outside of their musical responsibilities.

The principal factor that contributed to the tremendous increase in the number of Union bands during the early months of the war was the manner in which the volunteer regiments were raised. In 1861 almost anyone who could raise a regiment could attach the title of colonel to his name and become its commanding officer. One sure way of obtaining sufficient recruits to fill a regiment was to procure the services of a fine band, at extra expense if necessary. The presence of a military band was a strong inducement to the citizens to enlist in a particular regiment.

The best source for trained bandsmen was, of course, the numerous bands that were already established in the towns and cities across the land. By mid-1861 competition to enlist these bands had become fierce as the supply dwindled. In densely populated states, such as Pennsylvania, Massachusetts, and New York, which were required to provide large numbers of volunteers, colonels vied with each other to secure the services of good bands for their regiments. For example, the Ringgold Cornet Band of Reading, Pennsylvania, continued to receive invitations to join newly organized regiments even after most of its members had joined the volunteer army. In late summer of 1861, Colonel W.W.H. Davis invited the Ringgold Band to join his regiment and he guaranteed that the musicians would be paid $30 per man per month with "the officers making up the deficiency of the Government pay." At the same time that the Ringgold Band was voting on Colonel Davis' offer, it considered a similar proposition from Colonel Sickels of the 3rd Pennsylvania Regiment who had upped the ante. Sickels offered to pay each bandsman $40 a month, an amount roughly double the pay scale of the army.[1] Apparently neither offer was accepted.

By the closing months of 1861, the Federal government had begun to experience financial difficulties caused by the war, and it soon realized that it could no longer afford the luxury of permitting volunteer regiments to have bands. Of course, the government had no one to blame but itself for the large number of bands in the army. When the War Department established its plan of organization for the volunteer forces in May of 1861, it had specified that infantry regi-

---

(1) Ringgold Cornet Band Ledger, entry dated Sept. 9, 1861. The ledger is in the archives of the Ringgold Band of Reading, Penn.

ments were to have "24 musicians for [the] band."[2] A majority of the regiments mustered into service during the first six months of the war went into training camp with bands. An inspection of some of the camps by the U.S. Sanitary Commission in September and October of 1861 revealed that 143 out of the 200 regiments examined (nearly 75%) had bands. In its report to the government, the Commission noted that although most of the bands were of average ability, the soldiers took a great deal of pride in their musical units.[3]

It is difficult to ascertain the exact number of Federal bandsmen serving with volunteer regiments during the first six months of war. Some bands were mustered in with fewer than 24 musicians, others exceeded that number. Using the Sanitary Commission's figure of 143 bands and a figure of 20 for the average number of musicians in a band, we can roughly calculate that there were 2,800 regimental bandsmen serving with the Federal army in the fall of 1861. Secretary of War Cameron recommended to President Lincoln that "the employment of regimental bands should be limited; the proportion of musicians now allowed by law being too great, and their usefulness not at all commensurate with their heavy expense."[4] Benjamin F. Larned, Paymaster-General of the Army, estimated that the Federal government would save about $5 million annually if it abolished regimental bands.[5]

The first adverse order affecting regimental bands was issued by the War Department in October of 1861. The order forbade the mustering in of new regimental bands and prohibited the enlistment of bandsmen to fill vacancies. It further directed that all members of bands who were not musicians be discharged by their commanders (apparently there were abuses in this area).[6]

The major blow to regimental bands came in July of 1862 when the War Department issued General Order No. 91 directing that all regimental bandsmen be mustered out of service within 30 days. Musicians who were recruited from infantry companies to serve in bands (some bandsmen were recruited in this manner), were ordered to be transferred back to their units. Bandsmen who had been mustered in as musicians to be discharged from the service or, with their own consent, to be transferred to brigade bands.[7]

Although General Order 91 greatly reduced the number of bands in the Federal army, it did not eliminate them altogether. Section six of the order provided for the establishment of smaller bands—16 musicians maximum plus a bandleader—at the bri-

gade level (a brigade consisted of three or more regiments). A number of bandleaders who were discharged in August of 1862 went home for a time, reorganized their musical units, and then re-enlisted with their men to form brigade bands. Because many of the best musicians ended up in these bands, the net result of the reduction of bands was an improvement in the overall quality of playing.

Although regimental bands were officially abolished in the summer of 1862, some regiments were able to retain their bands after that time by re-enlisting the musicians as combatants, then detailing the men to the band. (In battle, some of these bandsmen were obliged to trade their instruments for muskets.) By this means some brigades had regimental bands as well as a brigade band for the duration of the war. Butkin estimates that at least 100 brigade bands served in the Federal army during the Civil War, and that more than 50 regimental bands served after the issuance of General Order 91 which officially abolished regimental bands.[8]

CONFEDERATE ARMY BANDS

Confederate army regulations promulgated in 1861 stipulated that: "When it is desired to have bands of music for regiments, there will be allowed for each, sixteen privates to act as musicians, in addition to the chief musicians authorized by law. . . ." The Regulations also state that "the musicians of the band . . . will be instructed as soldiers and liable to serve in the ranks on any occasion."[9]

Although information about Confederate bands is sparse, there are sufficient references in historical sources to indicate that bands were more prevalent in the Southern army than is generally believed. For example, a Confederate bandsman who participated in a grand review of A.P. Hill's entire Third Corps in September of 1863 reported that "there were seventeen bands in the field."[10] The report mentioned an eighteenth band (which was not in the review for some unspecified reason). These 18 bands existed in

(2) *The War of the Rebellion: A Compilation of the Official Records of the Union and Confederate Armies* (Washington, D.C.: Government Printing Office, 1899), Series III, Vol. 1, pp. 151-52.

.(3) *A Report to the Secretary of War of the Operation of the Sanitary Commission* (Washington, D.C.: McGill & Witherow, Printers, 1861), p. 41.

(4) "Report of the Secretary of War," dated Dec. 1, 1861, Daily National Intelligencer, Dec. 7, 1861, p. 2.

(5) *The War of the Rebellion*, Series III, Vol. 1, p. 728.

(6) *The War of the Rebellion*, Series III, Vol. 1, pp. 596-97.

(7) *The War of the Rebellion*, Series III, Vol. 2, pp. 270-79.

(8) *Union Bands of the Civil War*, pp. 74, 76.

(9) *Army Regulations Adopted for the Use of the Army of the Confederate States* (New Orleans: Bloomfield and Steel, 1861) p. 6.

(10) Cited in Harry H. Hall, *A Johnny Reb Band From Salem* (Raleigh: The North Carolina Centennial Commission, 1963), p. 63.

just one corps of Lee's army. This corps had sustained terrible losses at Gettysburg two months earlier, but still maintained its bands in spite of the Confederacy's manpower shortage. In another first-hand report, a British officer who had visited a Confederate Army headquarters wrote that "almost every regiment had a small band with brass instuments."[11] Rebel bands were generally smaller than Union Army bands and their instrumentation more varied.

From what is known about rebel bands, it would appear that North Carolina provided a goodly number of bands and trained bandsmen for the Confederate Army, possibly more than any other southern state. By 1861 North Carolina had several Moravian communities flourishing within its borders. The Moravians had had a long tradition of instrumental music performance in their homes, churches, and communities dating back to the mid-eighteenth century. When the Governor of North Carolina called for volunteers to serve the cause of the Confederacy, Moravians were ready to do their duty. The Moravian community of Salem (now Winston-Salem) provided two bands of musicians for volunteer regiments. One group became the Regimental Band of the 21st North Carolina Troops, Frank W. Carmichael, Leader, and the other became the Regimental Band of the 26th North Carolina Troops, Sam T. Mickey, Leader. The community of Bethania also provided a group of trained musicians (mostly Moravians) who formed the nucleus of the 33rd North Carolina band. At least a half dozen additional North Carolina regiments are known to have been successful in recruiting and organizing bands within the state. These include the 4th, 25th, 27th, 44th, 54th, and 55th Regiments. The musicians of the 4th North Carolina band, which was led by Edward B. Neave, were from Salisbury. Before the Civil War this group had been known as the Salisbury Brass Band.

In Virginia, the Mountain Saxhorn Band of Staunton joined the 5th Virginia Infantry and became known as the Stonewall Brigade Band. The Valley Brass Band of Virginia, which was organized before the war, enlisted as a group and served with the 48th Infantry Regiment; these bandsmen were present at Appomattox where they, along with other Confederate musicians, were permitted to retain their instruments and music after Lee surrendered. The Armory Band of Richmond, which had been attached to the city's Public Guard from 1845 to 1860, became the 1st Virginia Regiment Band. In the 1850s, the old Armory Band had enjoyed great popularity under the leadership of James B. Smith, an accomplished keyed bugler. Smith led the 1st Regiment Band throughout

its 12-month enlistment during the war (April 1861 to April 1862). The band reportedly acquired a "splendid reputation" among Confederate troops stationed at Manassas Junction. Lieutenant William M. Owen, adjutant of the famous Washington Artillery from New Orleans, a unit that camped beside the 1st Virginia Regiment at Manassas, wrote:

> He [Colonel Moore, Commander of the 1st Virginia Regiment] had an excellent band, better, I think, than ours, and each gave excellent music at guard-mounting and dress parade. "Listen to the Mocking-bird" was the favorite air of the Virginians.[12]

The Americus Brass Band of Georgia joined the Confederate Army early in the war and served as the Regimental Band of the 4th Georgia Volunteers. Organized by Professor Louis Zitterbart in May of 1860, the Americus Brass Band was considered one of the best bands in the state. After a concert given by the band in the spring of 1861, a reporter for the Augusta Chronicle wrote: "This excellent band . . . has afforded our citizens great gratification during their sojourn to this city, by the very music they have given us. They are capital performers."[13] The 4th Georgia band was mustered in with 12 musicians. Additional musicians were recruited from the companies of the regiment to increase the band's size to 18. After serving with distinction in several campaigns (including Gettysburg), the 4th Georgia band was present during the final day at Appomattox.

At least three South Carolina regiments are known to have had bands—the 14th, 15th, and 25th. The latter regimental band was composed of German musicians who had been playing together for ten years prior to the Civil War. As skilled performers, these musicians were able to perform difficult operatic arrangements with relative ease in their concerts for the soldiers.[14]

Mississippi units that are known to have had bands include the 3rd, 12th, 16th, and 43rd regiments. The band of the 16th Mississippi Volunteers, reputedly one of the best musical groups in the Confederate Army, was led by William H. Hartwell, an accomplished musician, composer, and arranger. After the war Hartwell was for a time professor of music at Madison College, Sharon, Mississippi.[15]

Although fewer in number, military bands were

---

(11) "A Month's Visit to the Confederate Headquarters," *Blackwood's Edinburg Magazine*, American edition, Vol. LVI, January-June 1863, p. 23.

(12) Cited in Louis H. Manarin and Lee A. Wallace, Jr., *Richmond Volunteers 1861-1865* (Richmond: Westover Press, 1969), p. 194.

(13) Historical notes included with record album titled *Fourth Georgia Regimental Band; To The Traditions of the South*, privately produced, 1980.

(14) Hall, p. 92.

(15) Hall, p. 63.

organized with volunteer units in Tennessee (28th Infantry), Kentucky (4th Infantry), Louisiana, Texas, and Alabama. One brigade from Alabama boasted two or three very good bands which, according to a soldier's account, regularly entertained the troops with "the best kind of martial music."[16]

To date, no one has ventured a guess as to number of bands and bandsmen that served with the Confederate Army during the Civil War. Although estimates for the Union Army vary considerably, Bufkin's conservative figures of 500 bands and 9,000 bandsmen appear to be close to the mark. Extrapolating from these figures and what is currently known about Confederate bands, we estimate that the South fielded no more that 125 bands and 1,600 bandsmen. More accurate figures will have to wait further research.

BAND SIZE AND INSTRUMENTATION

Although the Federal government authorized volunteer regiments to have bands of up to 24 musicians during the early months of the war, seldom does one see more than 16 musicians in photographs of Yankee bands (16 was the maximum number allowed in brigade bands after July 1862). Confederate bands varied in size from as few as eight to as many as 16, the maximum number allowed by law. Of course, the deprivations of war often affected the personnel of bands in both armies.

It is difficult to determine the instrumentation of Civil War bands by looking at photographs. For one thing, it is usually impossible to ascertain if everyone who played in a particular band was present when the picture was taken. Furthermore, while it may be possible to identify specific instruments and the number of players who played those instruments, usually there is no way to tell which part was played by which player or whether or not a player doubled a part. A more fruitful method of determining the instrumentation of military bands is to look at the music used by the musicians.

Examination of Civil War era part-books and published brass band journals reveals that the "basic instrumentation" of a fully instrumented brass band was: first and second E-flat cornet (or saxhorn), first and second B-flat cornet (or saxhorn), first and second E-flat alto horn, first and second B-flat tenor horn, B-flat baritone, E-flat bass, side drum, bass drum, and cymbals. To this well-balanced instrumentation, some music adds parts for solo alto horn, B-flat bass, and, occasionally, one or more of the following woodwind instruments: D-flat piccolo, C flute, E-flat soprano clarinet, and B-flat soprano clarinet. Although there were several excellent Union bands which had a mixture of woodwind, brass, and percussion instruments, large bands with woodwind sections were exceptions to the rule of the day which was the small 14 to 16 piece brass band.

DUTIES OF BANDSMEN

Military bandsmen had two kinds of responsibilities during the Civil War. In addition to playing for dress parades, guard mount, morning colors, reviews, funerals, and the like, band musicians served as stretcher bearers (or medical corpsmen, as they would be called today). When their units were engaged in battle, bandsmen often put away their instruments and assisted regimental and brigade surgeons with amputations and other medical operations in field hospitals set up behind the lines. They also helped to transport and care for the wounded and bury the dead.

Julius A. Leinbach of the 26th North Carolina Band vividly described what it was like to be a bandsman during the battle of Gettysburg. Leinbach's account was based on his war diary. After describing the regiment's experience on the first day of battle (July 1, 1863), when nearly three-fourths of the men were killed or wounded, Leinbach continued:

It was therefore with heavy hearts that we went about our duties caring for the wounded. We worked until 11 o'clock that night. . . . At 3 o'clock [the next morning] I was up again and at work. The second day our regiment was not engaged [because casualties were so high], but we were busily occupied all day in our sad tasks [of caring for the wounded]. While thus engaged, in the afternoon, we were sent . . . to play for the men [who were not injured], thus perhaps, [to] cheer them somewhat. . . . We accordingly went to the regiment and found the men much more cheerful than we were ourselves. We played for some time, the 11th N.C. Band playing with us, and the men cheered us lustily. Heavy cannonading was going on at the time, though not in our immediate front. We learned afterwards, from Northern papers, that our playing had been heard across the lines and caused wonder that we should play while fighting was going on around us. Some little while after we left, a bomb struck and exploded very close to the place where we had been standing, no doubt having been intended for us. We got back to camp after dark and found many men in need of [medical] attention. Some of those whom we had tried to care for during the day had died during our absence. . . . We continued our administrations until late at night and early the next morning.

Leinbach summarized the terrible events he had witnessed at Gettysburg by noting that out of 800 men of the 26th Regiment who went into battle on July 1, only 83 were left to answer roll call on the morning of July 4th: "Surely this regiment had done its

(16) Cited in Bell I. Wiley, *The Life of Johnny Reb* (New York: Doubleday & Co., Inc., 1971), p. 156.

full duty—was baptized in blood, and well deserved the appellation 'The Bloody Twenty-sixth'.[17]

Although most Civil War bandsmen were officially classified as noncombatants, they were on rare occasions ordered to play their instruments in the heat of battle. During the battle of Dinwiddie Court House, for example, General Sheridan rounded up all of the bands under his command and put them on the firing line along with his infantry; he then ordered them to loudly play their gayest tunes and to "never mind if a bullet goes through a trombone or even a trombonist, now and then."[18] In the same battle, a Confederate band was ordered to the front to counteract the fervor that was generated by a Federal band; the commander of the 1st Maine Cavalry reported:

> Our band came up from the rear and cheered and animated our hearts by its rich music; ere long a rebel band replied by giving us southern airs; with cheers from each side in encouragement of its own band, a cross-fire of the "Star Spangled Banner," "Yankee Doodle," and "John Brown," mingled with "Dixie" and the "Bonnie Blue Flag."[19]

A more delightful aspect of being a band musician during the Civil War was that of playing to entertain the troops. Twilight concerts for the soldiers and serenades for high ranking officers and their visiting wives were performed regularly by the bands when their units were camped. On these occasions the bandsmen demonstrated their musical skills by playing some of their most difficult pieces, often the latest operatic selections arranged for band by eminent bandleaders.

Civil War soldiers derived great pleasure from the evening camp concerts given by their bands, and they expressed their appreciation in letters to their relatives. For example, one infantryman with the 24th Massachusetts Regiment wrote home in April of 1862:

> I don't know what we should have done without our band. It is acknowledged by everyone to be the best in the division. Every night about sun down [Patrick] Gilmore gives us a spendid concert, playing selections from the operas and some very pretty marches, quicksteps, waltzes and the like, most of which are composed by himself or by Zohler, a member of his band. . . . Thus you see we get a great deal of *new* music, notwithstanding we are off here in the woods.[20]

When Union and Confederate troops were camped in proximity of each other, the soldiers of one army could sometimes hear the music played by the bands of the other army. Writing of his experiences in the Confederate Army, Lieutenant Lot D. Young of Kentucky wrote:

> [From our position] we could see extending for miles his [Sherman's] grand encampment of infantry and artillery . . . [which presented] the greatest panorama I ever beheld. Softly and sweetly the music from their bands as they played the national airs were wafted up and over the summit of the mountain. Somehow, some way, in some inexplicable and unseen manner, "Hail Columbia," "America" and "The Star Spangled Banner" sounded sweeter than I had ever before heard them and filled my soul with feelings that I could not describe or forget. It haunted me for days, but never shook my loyalty to the Stars and Bars. . . .[21]

Military bands and bandsmen served an important role duing the Civil War, bringing much pleasure and enjoyment into the oftentimes dull and routine life of the ordinary soldier. When Federal authorities were considering the elimination of regimental bands in 1862 because the cost was too great, Alonzo Quint, Chaplain of the 2nd Massachusetts Regiment, protested:

> Those who advocate this [the discharge of regimental bands] cannot have an idea of their value among soldiers. I do not know anything particular of the science or practice of music . . . but I see the effects of a good band, like ours, continually. It scatters the dismal part of camp life; gives new spirit to the men jaded by or on a march; wakes up their enthusiasm. Could you see our men, when, of an evening, our band comes out and plays its sweet stirring music, you would say, if retrenchment must come, let it be somewhere else. . . . let the men have their music.[22]

(17) "Scenes at The Battle of Gettysburg" by J.A. Leinbach. Paper read before the Wachovia Historical Society. Published in Bernard J. Pfohl, *The Salem Band* (Winston-Salem: privately printed, 1953), pp. 78-80.

(18) Bruce Catton, *A Stillness at Appomattox* (New York: Pocket Books, 1953), pp. 388-89.

(19) Edward P. Tobie, *History of the First Maine Cavalry 1861-1865* (Boston: Press of Emery & Hughes, 1887), p. 402.

(20) Bell I. Wiley, *The Life of Billy Yank* (New York: Doubleday & Company, Inc., 1971), p. 158. The historian of the 24th Massachusetts Regiment wrote of Gilmore's band: "As nearly perfect as the musicians were in their work, they could produce discords, as when their application for furlough was disapproved. Then in their way across the parade ground, there came from their brazen instruments notes that no one would believe them capable of blowing, but the spell disappeared and harmony as of old prevailed." Alfred S. Roe, *The Twenty-fourth Regiment, Massachusetts Volunteers, 1861-1865* (Worcester, Massachusetts: Twenty-fourth Veteran Association, 1907), pp. 412-13.

(21) L.D. Young, *Reminiscences of a Soldier of the Orphan Brigade* (Paris, Kentucky: privately printed, n.d.), p. 76.

(22) Alonzo H. Quint, *The Potomac and the Rapidan, 1861-3* (Boston: Crosby and Nichols, 1864), p. 96.

Top: "The Saxonia Quick Step, as performed by the Boston Cornet Band. Composed and respectfully dedicated to Prof. A. Bond by George W. Lyon" (Boston: Henry Tolman, 1849). Alonzo Bond is shown here with his E-flat upright saxhorn which has three Vienna twin-piston valves. Courtesy of Kurt Stein.

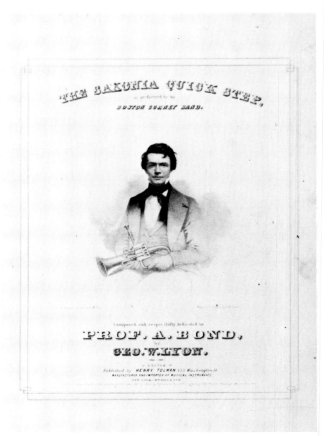

Bottom left: "Reynolds' Quick-step by Harvey B. Dodworth" (New York: Firth, Hall & Pond, c. 1849). Dodworth is seen here on the right with his OTS soprano saxhorn presenting the music to Reynolds. Courtesy of Kurt Stein.

Bottom right: "Guadalquiver Quick Step, composed and respectfully dedicated to Captain John S. Van Schaick of the Troy Citizen's Corps by Edward P. Jones [right], Leader of the Watervliet Arsenal Cornet Band" (New York: Firth, Pond & Co., 1849). Courtesy of Kurt Stein.

"Henry's Polka as played by Henry's United Silver Band. Composed by John A. Janke" (Philadelphia: Wm. F. Duffy & Co., 1854). We have been unable to find any information on this band or its leader, who is shown here with his E-flat upright saxhorn. Courtesy of Kurt Stein.

Handbill announcing a concert by the 22nd New York Regiment Band, F.B. Helmsmuller, Conductor, that was given a week after the Gettysburg battle. Authors' collection.

GRAND
CONCERT!

IN BEHALF OF THE

HEROES OF GETTYSBURG,

At the Court House, Harrisburg,

ON SATURDAY, JULY 11, 1863.

MILITARY BAND

Of the 22d Regiment N. G. N. Y. S.,

F. B. Helmsmüller, Conductor.

PROGRAMME--PART I.

1. TWENTY-SECOND REGIMENT PARADE MARCH.
2. GRAND OVERTURE—" Nabuco," .... VERDI.
3. DUETTO   I would that My Love," .... MENDELSSOHN.
   (For two Cornets a' Piston.)
4. QUARTETTS FROM THE OPERA "RIGOLETTO," .... VERDI
   (For Cornet Band.)
5. HINKLEY GALOP .... HELMSMUELLER.

PART II.

1. INTRODUCTION—Cavatina, (Shadow dance,) from the
   Opera " Le Pardon de Ploermel." .... MEYERBEER.
2. "IL BACIO "—Arietta in forme de Valse .... ARDITTI.
3. GENERAL COUCH'S GRAND MARCH .... HELMSMUELLER.
4. BOLERO—from " Vespers Siciliennes " .... VERDI.
   (For Cornet a' Piston.)
5. { A. BALLAD—When this Cruel is Over .... TUCKER.
   { B.   "   Kingdom Coming .... WORK.
      NATIONAL AIRS.

Printed at the " PATRIOT AND UNION " Steam Job Office, Harrisburg.

Cover to an 1864 publication of brass band music (marches, polkas, quicksteps, operatic airs, popular songs, etc.) composed by David L. Downing. Authors' collection.

DOWNING'S
JOURNAL OF MILITARY MUSIC,

FOR BRASS BANDS.

Arranged for TEN Instruments, namely: 2 Eb CORNETS, 2 Bb CORNETS, 2 Bb TENORS, 2 Eb TENORS, 1 BARITONE, 1 CONTRABASS. With additional parts for SIDE DRUM, BASS DRUM, 3d Eb TENOR, and Bb BASS.

(N. B.—If a 3d Eb Cornet be added, it will play the same as the 3d Eb Tenor.)

By D. L. DOWNING, of Dodworth's Band, New-York.

CONTENTS.

No. 1. Review March.	No. 7.
2. Troop No. 1.	8.
3. Port Royal Schottisch.	9.
4. Sprites Frolic Polka.	10.
5.	11.
6.	12.

The music contained in this Journal will consist of original Marches, Polkas, Quicksteps, Operatic Airs, etc. Also the popular songs of the day will, from time to time, be added to the list. The pieces will be of the character and style required by Professional Bands for general business purposes, calculated to advance all who play, either for improvement or pleasure, but not of great difficulty, so that nearly all bands can perform them creditably. The experience of the times must have shown to all musicians, that bold, dashing, and spirited music is required for military purposes; and that the old sing-song style of the past is out of place entirely. The author hopes to be able to meet this new want successfully, and with that end in view, will introduce nothing but such music as, in his opinion, will be acceptable to the public.

Price $1 per Single Copy; Six Copies, $5.

Published by WILLIAM A. POND & CO., 547 Broadway, New-York.

Entered according to Act of Congress, in the year 18.. by WM. A. POND & CO., in the Clerk's Office of the District Court of the United States for the Southern District of New-York.

E-flat cornetist, 11th Corps, c. 1864. His OTS saxhorn probably was made by William Seefeldt of Philadelphia. Quite often the tubing configuration of a brass instrument identifies its maker. Authors' collection.

Unidentified Federal musician with E-flat upright bass and music. Most Civil War bandsmen played from small part-books that contained arrangements copied out by hand. Courtesy of Jeremy Rowe.

New Hampshire bandsman with circular B-flat cornet. The mechanical linkage rotary valves on his instrument indicate that it probably was made in Europe around 1860. Courtesy of Robert Hazen.

Regimental bandsmen of the 4th Rhode Island Volunteer Infantry, c. 1861. The musician on the right is holding a B-flat soprano saxhorn with three Paine rotary valves. This quick-action valve design was patented by Thomas D. Paine of Woonsocket, Rhode Island, in 1848. Paine is the earliest known maker to use string linkge to turn the rotors of valves. Authors' collection.

BOSTON BRASS BAND.

Lithograph of the Boston Brass Band, early 1850s. All of the brass players in this 16-piece band are using OTS horns. Note the three trombonists depicted to the left of the snare drummer. From *Gleason's Pictorial Drawing Room Companion,* August 9, 1851.

HOWARD'S QUICK STEP,

PERFORMED BY THE BOSTON BRASS BAND AND RESPECTFULLY DEDICATED

E.B. FLAGG ESQ?
BY
FRANK HOWARD
(Of Dumbolton's Ethiopian Serenaders)
& Arranged from their most
FAVOURITE MELODIES.
BOSTON.
Published by STEPHEN W. MARSH, No 5 Adams House
Piano Forte Maker & Music Dealer.

"Howard's Quick Step. Performed by the Boston Brass Band and respectfully dedicated to E.B. Flagg, Esq., by Frank Howard of the Dumbolton's Ethiopian Serenaders" (Boston: Stephen W. Marsh, 1849). Eben Flagg, who is shown here with his E-flat keyed bugle, led the Boston Brass Band for eight years during the late 1840s and early 1850s. Courtesy of Kurt Stein.

Unidentified officer and bandleader, late 1860s. The rotary valves on his instrument were designed and patented by Isaac Fiske in 1866. The valve rotors are placed at the bottom of the instrument and are turned with string linkages; however, the strings are attached to vertical rods which are passed up through cylinders and are capped with finger buttons. The cylinders have return springs for the rods. Courtesy of Robert Hazen.

Unidentified Civil War era cornetist. The tubing configuration on his rare three-valve B-flat cornet is quite unusual. Notice the large water valve positioned at the bottom of one of the circles of tubing. Courtesy of Robert Hazen.

Unidentified musician and Civil War casualty, c. late 1860s. The shape of the maker's shield on the bell of his B-flat or A-flat trumpet indicates that the instrument was probably made in New York. Courtesy of Robert Hazen.

Militia bandsman from Indiana, c. 1870. His rare bell front alto horn in E-flat has three string rotary valves and side action levers. The photo backmark reads: "From album belonging to Niblick family of Decatur, Ind." Courtesy of Robert Hazen.

Unidentified bandsman with B-flat bass. The musician's sword and shoulder epaulets indicate that he is an officer and possibly a bandleader. His four-valve saxhorn was converted from an OTS to a bell upright instrument. Courtesy of Robert Hazen.

Charles A. Carter, "IInd E-flat Tuba," 13th Wisconsin Infantry. This photo was taken in Huntsville, Alabama in 1865. Carter's OTS bass saxhorn is shown and described on page 24 (right side). Courtesy of William Gladstone.

E-flat bass player from Poughkeepsie, New York, c. 1865. His OTS saxhorn has three Perinet piston valves. Perinet valves were not widely used in this country until well after the Civil War. Authors' collection.

Levi Palmer, 1st Maine Heavy Artillery, c. 1862. His four-valve instrument is shown and described on page 24 (left side). Authors' collection.

The Aurora Colony Pioneer Band at Portland, Oregon, July 1876. courtesy of the Oregon Historical Society, Portland.

George J. Wolfer playing his ophicleide in 1917. When this photograph was taken, Wolfer may have been the oldest surviving ophicleide player from the brass band era. He was a member of the Aurora Colony, Oregon. Courtesy of the Oregon Historical Society, Portland.

Mounted brass band performing at a reception for Brig-adier-General Corcoran hosted by Mayor Opdyke and the citizens of New York at Castle Garden. From *Frank Leslie's Illustrated Newspaper,* September 6, 1862. Courtesy of Jon Newsom and Library of Congress.

The precariousness of playing an instrument while riding on a horse was humorously described by New Hampshire bandsman John C. Linehan: "[The Fisherville Cornet Band of Penacook, New Hampshire] secured and maintained a reputation that placed it among the best musical organizations of the state. It accompanied the Pioneer Engine company to the last great firemen's muster in Manchester in 1859, and marched . . . in the great torchlight procession in Boston in October, 1860. . . . The best tribute paid the band at the same time was its selection to perform service for the Governor's Horse Guards, one of the most stylish military organizations ever recruited in New Hampshire. . . .

"Their engagement by the Horse Guards, although a matter of pride, was nevertheless an occasion for dismay, for the boys for the first time in their lives had to play on horseback. As nearly all of them were novices in this direction the outlook was serious, for it is a question if there were half a dozen of the number that had ever straddled a horse. When the proposition was first broached in the band room, one of the saddest looking men was the leader, Loren Currier. He said he would vote to accept on one condition, and that was if a horse could be secured large enough to have them all ride together and give him a place in the middle. The proposition was, however, accepted, and for three or four weeks the flat on the Boscawen side looked like a western ranch, surrounded by a lot of tenderfoots playing the part of cowboys, for it was up there the boys went to break in their steeds. It was a moving sight (the moving was all towards the ground, however), and the bucking broncos of the Wild West show furnished no more sport, while it lasted, than did the gallant equestrians of the Fisherville band while trying to train their horses to march and wheel by fours. But they finally overcame all obstacles, and a proud lot they were when they made their first appearance on Main street in Concord, at the head of the gorgeous squadron of hussars. This was in the spring of 1861, a year full of historic memories." (D. Arthur Brown, *History of Penacook, N.H.* [Concord, N.H.: The Rumford Press, 1902], pp. 248-49.)

Lorenzo (Loren) M. Currier, New Hampshire band-leader and cornetist, c. 1860s. He led the Fisherville Cornet Band from 1859 to 1861. (During the war he played E-flat cornet with the 3rd N.H. Regiment Band and the 2nd Brigade Band, 10th Corps.) John Linehan, who had been a member of the Fisherville Cornet Band, recalled: "The advent of Loren M. Currier as Leader [of the Fisherville Band] opened a new source of pleasure, for a better story teller never lived, and the recollections of the happy hours spent during recess at rehearsals listening to him . . . is enough to make one wish he was a boy again." Authors' collection.

Band of the 114th Pennsylvania Volunteer Infantry (Collis' Zouaves), Frank Rauscher, bandleader, c. 1861-62. Courtesy of Jon Newsom and the Library of Congress.

According to Rauscher, the uniform adopted for the 114th Pa. regiment and band was that of the French Zouave d'Afrique—red pants, Zouave jacket, white leggings, blue sash around the waist, and white turban. The material for the uniforms was imported from France, and special arrangements were made to secure a sufficient supply for the duration of the war. Concerning the band, Rauscher wrote that "about one year before the war broke out, a number of young men formed a cornet band in Germantown. As instrumental musicians, they were amateurs and beginners, but with a fair knowledge of music as vocalists, by close application they made rapid progress. . . . When the band was started [Capt. F.A. Elliott of Germantown] became a helpful friend of the project, subscribing liberally toward procuring instruments, and afterward assisted in supplying the members with uniforms. . . . Subsequent events . . . proved to have been a good policy on the part of the officers to secure a band, . . . it became a prime factor and one of the most efficient aids in maintaining discipline." (Frank Rauscher, *Music on the March, 1862-65, with the Army of the Potomac, 114th Regt. P.V., Collis' Zouaves,* [Philadelphia: Wm. F. Fell & Co., 1892], pp. 11-14.)

Ambulance drill at army headquarters near Brandy Station, March 1864. Bandsmen were trained in the techniques of transporting and caring for the wounded. They were also taught first aid skills. The Zouave soldiers depicted in this practice drill may have been members of Frank Rauscher's band of the 114th Pennsylvania Infantry. Courtesy of Jon Newsom and the Library of Congress.

In an interview that was published in the *American Art Journal,* July 17, 1880, bandleader Harvey Dodworth recalled this wartime incident: "Our band went out with the Seventy-first Regiment N.G.S.N.Y., and was with them at Bull Run. . . . During a lull in the engagement, I busied myself in seeing what I could do for the wounded, and in giving what I could to our own boys and the rebels alike. I came across one poor fellow, a 'reb' Lieutenant, who had suffered a frightful wound, the shattering of one leg at the ankle. He was in a very great pain, and I stopped the flow of blood as well as I could, gave him a drink of water, carried him to the shelter of a fence, and made him as easy as possible, to await the surgeons. As he began to feel a little relief from his great pain, his eyes rested on my legs, and then slowly wandered up until his gaze reached my bugle hanging at my side, when he brightened up, and with an air of awakened interest, asked feebly: 'Mister, is that an E flat?' I said that it was. 'Ah,' he said, 'I used to play that.' He told me that he belonged to the 'Louisiana Tigers.' Soon afterward circumstances over which we had no control, caused us to take a lively interest in moving from there with some degree of precipitancy, and I never knew what became of the poor fellow."

Unidentified musician from Springfield, Massachusetts. Authors' collection.

Bandsman, 34th New York Regiment, c. 1861. Authors' collection.

Federal musician, c. 1861. Courtesy of George M. Cress.

Unidentified bandsman from Maine. His E-flat alto sax-horn was made by E.G. Wright around 1862. Authors' collection.

E-flat bass player Joseph Kingsbury, c. 1861. His unusual upright saxhorn with five string rotary valves probably was made by Samuel Graves around 1855. Kingsbury was a member of the Boston Brigade Band during the 1850s. Authors' collection.

Federal musician Frederick Loehmann with his E-flat soprano saxhorn, c. 1861. This photo was taken in Little Rock, Arkansas. Courtesy of Robert Hazen.

Signal Corps musician with his E-flat soprano saxhorn. A Matthew Brady photograph from the U.S. Army Military History Institute, Carlisle, Pennsylvania.

Unidentified bandsman from Pennsylvania with his E-flat bass saxhorn. Courtesy of Howard Hoffman.

Unidentified Union Army bandsman. Courtesy of Robert Hazen.

Militia bandsmen from New England, c. 1855. Their E-flat bass saxhorns have five string rotary valves. The leather pouches strapped to the musicians' belts were used to carry and protect small bandbooks. On the march, the musician would take his music from the pouch and place it in a music lyre on his instrument as needed. Courtesy Manchester (N.H.) Historic Association.

Young bandsman, 44th Regiment (unidentified state). Courtesy of Henry Deeks.

Musicians of the 4th Michigan Infantry Band, c. 1861-62. Courtesy of Robert Hazen.

Regimental bandsman, 4th Vermont Infantry, c. 1861-62. His E-flat alto saxhorn has a "pigtail" in the lead pipe which indicates that it probably was made in Boston. Courtesy of Wendell Lang, Jr.

Unidentified militia bandsman with B-flat tenor trombone, early 1870s. The slide trombone was not widely used by military bandsmen during the Civil War. After the war, however, the instrument gradually secured a firm position in the instrumentation of American bands. Note that the musician seems to be holding the trombone in his right hand instead of his left; this is an example of the image reversal of early photographs. Authors' collection.

Ohio bandsman with E-flat flugelhorn, early 1860s. Authors' collection.

G. Bower with his E-flat soprano saxhorn. From a composite photograph of Captain Rush's Brass Band, early 1860s. Authors' collection.

Daniel Hiram Chandler, the "father of band music" in Maine. For nearly two decades prior to the war, Chandler led the Portland Brass Band. In 1861 he and most of his band joined the 1st Maine Volunteer Infantry. Subsequently, they served with the bands of the 10th and 29th Regiments, and with the 25th Maine Brigade. Chandler was an accomplished keyed bugler, cornetist, and violinist. After the war, he led his own military band until he retired in 1885. Courtesy Maine Historical Society.

Principal musician, unknown New Hampshire regiment, c. 1861. His E-flat cornet, which has three side action rotary valves, probably was made by J. Lathrop Allen or by Allen & Hall. Authors' collection.

Military dress parade showing a brass band with OTS saxhorns and a drums section with two snare drums. Piano sheet music cover published by John Church Jr., Cincinnati, 1863. Lithograph by Ehrogtt, Forbirger & Co. Courtesy of Kurt Stein.

Manchester Band, Vermont, 1861. This 17-piece band is dressed in civilian frock coats, white duck trousers and forage caps or "kepis." The musicians in the second and third ranks are holding OTS alto, tenor, and bass saxhorns with Berliner valves. The bandsmen in the front rank are holding circular cornets with string rotary valves. Although circular horns pitched in E-flat and B-flat were common during the Civil War, rarely does one see an entire section of circular instruments. Courtesy Vermont Historical Museum, Montpelier.

Camp of the 67th New York Infantry with brass band and drum corps performing for what appears to be a parade review, c. 1861-62. Courtesy of Jon Newsom and the Library of Congress.

Unidentified Federal band serenading officers and their wives at the headquarters of General G.L. Hartstuff. Courtesy of Jon Newsom and the Library of Congress.

Band of the 44th Ohio Volunteer Infantry. This band was from Springfield, Ohio. Courtesy Ohio Historical Society.

6th Michigan Regiment Band at Camp McKim, Baltimore, Maryland. This band from Kalamazoo, Michigan, enlisted as a group in 1861. Their brass instruments included a mixture of upright and OTS saxhorns as well as bell front and circular cornets. Two of the circular horns have detachable bells. An instrument of this design could easily be converted to an OTS saxhorn by replacing the circular bell with one that pointed backward. Authors' collection.

Opposite: Bandsmen, 2nd Rhode Island Volunteer Infantry, c. 1861-62. Although this informal group photograph probably was taken without all of the bandsmen present, the instrumentation is balanced. The wind instruments are from left to right: bell front cornet, circular cornet, alto saxhorn, baritone horn, upright bass (with Berliner valves), and E-flat clarinet. The E-flat alto saxhorn depicted in the left foreground was converted from an OTS horn to an upright design. Note the pistol strapped to the clarinettist's side. Courtesy of Jon Newsom and the Library of Congress.

Civil War military bands were often required to perform with less than a full compliment of musicians. Pennsylvania bandsman J.C. Irwin wrote: "Today five of the band were reported sick. . . . But the general gave orders that the band must play for dress parade, or turn in our horns to the quartermaster, and to get muskets for them. The band came to the conclusion that the horns were worth more than the guns, so the trade was off, and when the time came the band was ready and reported for duty, and played 'Hail Columbia' five times during dress parade." (Allen D. Albert, *History of the Forty-fifth Regiment Pennsylvania Veteran Volunteer Infantry, 1861-1865* [Williamsport, Pennsylvania: Grit Publishing Company, 1912], p. 194.)

Opposite: 4th Regiment Band, Minnesota Volunteer Infantry at Huntsville, Alabama, c. 1864. Courtesy of the Minnesota Historical Society, St. Paul.

Historian William Bufkin provides this amusing story about the 2nd Minnesota Regiment Band. In May of 1863, the officers and men of the 2nd Minnesota Regiment decided to elevate their "bugle band" to the status of a brass band. With money provided by the regimental fund, a complete set of brass instruments was ordered from Cincinnati. Principal musician R.G. Rhodes was announced as bandleader, and "for the next few weeks the woods about the camp were full of practicing musicians." One of the bandmen reported that the musicians were making "fast headway" on their new instruments, and that they could play "Hail Columbia," "Yankee Doodle," and five other pieces. Apparently, infantryman Timothy H. Pendergast (who was not a musician) was not pleased with the idea of starting a brass band: "Misfortunes never come singly and on the next day a wagon load, more or less, of brass instruments, varying in size from a dinner horn to a cart wheel arrived for our band and peace fled, for the next two weeks the braying of the horns from one side of the camp would be answered by the braying of the mules from the other side. The poor mules no doubt thought another wagon train was parked over there. Whether the mules ever learned their mistake or the band boys . . . [ever] knew it was not a portion of their crowd answering them I cannot say, but presume neither were ever undeceived. . . ." (Cited in Bufkin, *Union Bands of the Civil War,* pp. 82-83.)

Band of the 33rd Massachusetts Regiment at Atlanta, Georgia, November, 1864. The band is pictured here with a detachment of infantry in front of the Atlanta Courthouse. Soon after this photograph was taken, the courthouse was destroyed along with most of the city. The 33rd Massachusetts band, led by Israel Smith, Jr., was regarded by many as the finest musical organization in Sherman's army. Prior to the Civil War, Smith led his own brass band in New Bedford, Massachusetts. Six members of the New Bedford band and several former members of the 12th Massachusetts band formed the nucleus of the 33rd Regiment band when it was mustered into service in August of 1862. The band served two and one-half years with the Union Army. Authors' collection.

Band of the 107th Colored Troops with matched set of OTS saxhorns, November 1863. The white bandleader pictured on the left is holding a bell front cornet. Negroes were not allowed to serve in Union bands until 1863, after the Emancipation Proclamation was issued. A Matthew Brady photograph from the Library of Congress.

Unidentified Union band with a matched set of OTS saxhorns. Authors' collection.

Band of the 102nd Ohio Volunteer Infantry, c. 1865. The image of this 17-piece band from Mansfield, Ohio, was made from two separate photographs placed side by side. Except for two circular cornets, an upright alto horn, and a trumpet, the band is equipped with OTS instruments. The single large E-flat bass pictured on the left probably was manufactured by the John F. Stratton Company. Courtesy of Jonathan Kerecz.

8th New York State Militia Band from Elmira, c. 1861. The Elmira Cornet Band was typical of many civilian musical organizations recruited into the volunteer armies of the North and South at the beginning of the Civil War. The OTS sax-horns pictured here appear to be both American and foreign made. A Matthew Brady photograph from the Library of Congress.

Unidentified Massachusetts regiment band, winter 1861-62. Although the photo backmark reads "25th M.S. Band Attleboro" (M.S. is an abbreviation for Massachusetts), the inscription probably was erroneously added by someone who once owned the photograph. The instrumentation of the 20-piece band depicted here, which includes a piccolo and an E-flat clarinet, does not match that of the 25th Massachusetts Regiment Band whose set of part-books have survived. Authors' collection.

Band of the 38th Illinois Infantry Regiment, Ringgold Barracks, Georgia, 1864. General William P. Carlin, pictured third from the left, had been the first commanding officer of the 38th Illinois. The musicians in the tree-loft bandstand are equipped with OTS saxhorns. Authors' collection.

10th Veteran Reserve Corps Band, Washington, D.C., April 1865. Courtesy of the Library of Congress.

23rd Ohio Volunteer Infantry Band at Charleston, West Virginia, 1863. Courtesy Rutherford B. Hayes Library, Fremont, Ohio.

1st Brigade Band, 3rd Division, 15th Army Corps, early 1864. Courtesy of the Chicago Public Library.

Unidentified Massachusetts regiment band, c. 1861. This 18-piece band has a piccolo, B-flat clarinet, and slide trombone in its instrumentation. The bandleader is standing in the left foreground with a cornet in his hand. Courtesy Henry Deeks.

Band of the 12th Indiana Infantry Regiment (Wallace's Zouaves), Scottsboro, Alabama, 1862. Led by Jacob K. Spence, this group had been the East Germantown Silver Cornet Band. The band served throughout the Civil War. In August of 1862 the bandsmen were captured in Richmond, Kentucky, and paroled shortly thereafter. Later in the war, they served as a brigade band and participated in the Grand Review down Pennsylvania Avenue, Washington, D.C., on May 24, 1865. The musicians are wearing typical mid-western Zouave uniforms. Courtesty of Fred Benkovic.

Militia band from Pennsylvania, c. 1863. This photo was taken at Chambersburg, Pennsylvania. Except for two circular cornets, most of the instruments are upright saxhorns with Berliner piston valves. Authors' collection.

Brass band from Monroeville, Ohio, c. 1865. The musicians in this small but well-balanced band are identified on the back of the photo as follows: (standing left to right) W. Davison, E-flat cornet, probably the bandleader; George Dickinson, 2nd B-flat cornet; A.A. Barnard, 1st E-flat alto; E.F. Kinsey, solo alto; S. Thompson, B-flat tenor; A.K. Pratt, E-flat bass; (seated left to right) A.D. Hersey, 1st B-flat cornet; C.L. Osborn, 2nd E-flat cornet; and J.A. Barnard, 2nd E-flat alto. Apparently the band's drummers were absent when the photograph was taken. Note the upturned cymbal attached to the bass drum; these two instruments were played by one person. Courtesy of Robert Hazen.

Members of the Leominster Brass Band who enlisted in 1861. These musicians served for 15 months with the band of the 1st Massachusetts Regiment, Militia Volunteers. During that time they were assigned to do picket duty along with other infantry soldiers and to care for the wounded (in addition to their musical chores). When their regimental band was discharged in 1862, several of the bandsmen reenlisted in the regular service. The musicians are from left to right: Andrew and Charles Tisdale, E-flat cornet; Charles A. Chase and Wooster F. Dodge, B-flat cornet; John Tisdale and Hibbard P. Pheeler, bass drum and cymbals; Loren L. Moore, tenor horn; Warren Gilchrest and George E. Tisdale, B-flat bass; and Joseph G. Eaton and Frank W. Lewis, E-flat bass. Courtesy of Fred Benkovic.

Regimental Band of the 13th Connecticut Infantry. When this regiment entered Federal service in March of 1862, it had no band because the bands of its home area had already enlisted with other units. However, when the regiment reached New Orleans, it was able to recruit a professional band led by Charles Bother. Signing up an existing band was a common practice, but this case was still unusual—the band had been in the Confederate Army before New Orleans fell. (It had served at the battle of Shiloh.) The instruments in this photo include a variety of OTS and upright saxhorns as well as bell front cornets and a trumpet. Authors' collection.

The Great Western Band of St. Paul, Minnesota, late 1860s. Courtesy of the Minnesota Historical Society, St. Paul.

Paul Maybery, leader of the new Great Western Band (established 1977), writes: "The original Great Western Band was organized in 1857 by businessman Russell C. Munger, a native of Connecticut. The small [brass] band soon became a very popular element in the social events of St. Paul, as evidenced by the numerous citations in the local press. Performing at nearly every public function in St. Paul, as well as travelling to other villages to provide the festivities, the band went on board the 'Frank Steel' to supply dancing and listening entertainment to those on the excursion to the Sioux Payment at Red Wood in 1861. Munger, a humorous character, added much levity and spontaneity to the long trip, and did much to promote the band's popularity in general. The band performed at fancy dress balls in the winter, political rallies, serenaded public officials on warm summer evenings, and participated in parades [on the 4th of July and St. Patrick's Day]. . . . In 1860, the band performed at old Fort Snelling in front of the commandant's house as part of the State Fair, at which 10,000 people attended. A year later it again appeared at the old fort, but this time to render field music for those soldiers enlisted in the first Minnesota Regiment of Volunteers, who were drilling in preparation for the war. This association of the Great Western Band with the military had existed long before the 'Great Rebellion,' as the band was the musical contingent of the Pioneer Guard, Minnesota's first home militia and subsequently Company A of the First Minnesota Regiment. . . . [During the Civil War, the Great Western Band] did its service at home in St. Paul, performing at benefits to raise money for hospital funds, parades to greet returning soldiers, and too frequently for the funerals of those lost in the war. . . . After a seven year tenure as leader of the band he organized, Russ Munger turned his duties over to George Seibert, [a musician and composer who led the band for many years after the Civil War]. . . ."

Town band from Massachusetts standing in front of an unidentified Civil War monument, early 1870s. A slide trombone and B-flat clarinet can be seen in the instrumentation of this post-war civilian band. Courtesy of Robert Hazen.

Unidentified Western brass band standing on the balcony of the Concert Hall, Central City, Colorado, 1872. The musicians, who may have just finished giving a concert, appear to have a matched set of OTS saxhorns. Courtesy of the Denver Public Library, Western History Department.

The Columbia Cornet Band of Pennsylvania, c. 1865-66. It is not known whether this band served during the Civil War. All of the brass players are using OTS saxhorns except the leader; he is using an upright saxhorn. The bass drum used by this band is shown and described on page 39. Authors' collection.

The Salem Cadet Band, late 1870s. The town of Salem, Massachusetts, has had community bands since the early nineteenth century. One of the first military bands in Massachusetts—the Brigade Band—was started in Salem in 1805-06; the Salem Brass Band was formed in 1837; the Salem Cornet Band was organized in 1852 (Patrick Gilmore led this band from 1855 to 1859); and the Salem Cadet Band was established in 1878 with Jean M. Missud as leader. The instrumentation of the Salem Cadet Band included trombones and woodwind instruments. Courtesy The Essex Institute, Salem, Massachusetts.

The Nemaha, Nebraska, Town Band, c. 1880s. The musicians, who are wearing European style uniforms, are from left to right: (seated) J. Lambert Melvin, George Fairbrother, George Dyer, Thomas Higgins, Tom Finch, Lance Jones; (standing) Bill Seid, unidentified, Charlie Dye, Fred Scoville, George Sanders, John E. Crother; the youngster seated on the floor is Worthy Frazier. All of the instruments have Perinet piston valves. Note the helicon tuba and valve trombones. Courtesy of Howard Browne.

Valve trombone in E-flat. Unsigned, c. 1875. German silver with three string rotary valves. Garofalo Collection.

Amateur brass bands such as the one pictured here continued to flourish in America to the end of the nineteenth century. In 1889 Leon Mead wrote: "The evolution of the present military or brass bands in the United States from the crude organizations of a quarter of a century ago has been rapid and marked. . . . Despite the humorous and sarcastic depreciation they have received from the press, the military bands of this country are doing a great educational work among the people. They dispense both the popular and higher class music of the day in remote sections where the inhabitants are unable to hear them at first hand, and without their local band they would perhaps never hear them at all. . . . In parts of the South good military bands are unknown, owing for one thing, to the dearth of acceptable reed and brass performers. Throughout the Eastern and Middle States hundreds of excellent brass bands exist, and then there are others which, to put it mildly, should not be taken seriously. . . . In the West many of the older bands have rosters of matchless musicians, and some of the more recently organized bands are forging ahead perfectionward with the usual Western vim." ("The Military Bands of the United States," Supplement to *Harper's Weekly*, Sept. 28, 1889, pp. 785-88.)

Sherman's Cornet Band of Winooski, Vermont, 1872. This photograph was taken in front of the Addison House in Middlebury, Vermont. In addition to upright basses and baritones and bell front cornets, the band has two side action rotary valve trombones that are similar to the instrument shown on page 33 (bottom). Courtesy Vermont Historical Museum, Montpelier.

3rd U.S. Infantry Band, Jefferson Barracks, Missouri, 1867. The instrumentation of this Regular Army band includes one trombone and a variety of upright, OTS, and bell front horns. The valve instruments have either Berliner piston or American string rotary valves. The snare drummer is using a rod tension side drum. Rod tension drums are rarely seen in early band photographs.

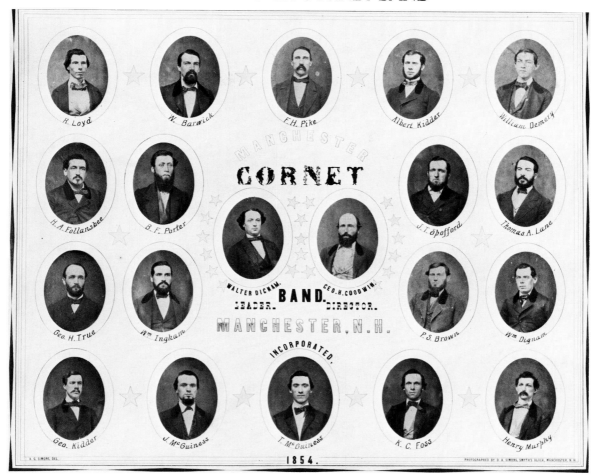

The Manchester Cornet Band in 1854. Courtesy The Manchester (N.H.) Historic Association.

Southeastern New Hampshire was a musically active region in the mid-nineteenth century. In addition to vocal groups such as the Hutchinson family singers of Milford, at least three well-documented brass bands were active in that part of the state—the Manchester Cornet Band (established in 1849), the Fisherville Cornet Band (founded in Penacook in 1858), and the 3rd New Hampshire Regiment Band (organized in Concord in 1861). The Manchester Band is the most interesting of the New Hampshire bands because its instrumentation changes can be traced in three sets of its manuscript part-books (dated 1849, 1852, and 1854) which now are part of the Walter P. Dignam Collection of the Manchester Historic Association. The instrumentation of the earliest band in Manchester consisted mainly of keyed bugles, ophicleides, and a few valved brass instruments. In 1852 the instrumentation was expanded to include trombones and ebor cornos (an alto register instrument). In 1854 the Manchester Band underwent yet another progressive change in instrumentation. Under the guidance of its leader, Walter Dignam, and director, George Goodwin, the newly incorporated "cornet" band converted to all-valve brass instruments. With new instrumentation and repertoire, the Manchester Cornet Band flourished in the late 1850s, giving greatly appreciated concerts year round.

In 1861 the Manchester Band enlisted with the 4th New Hampshire Volunteer Infantry. Early in the war, the band was stationed at Morris Island, South Carolina; later it was transferred to the Bermuda 100 battleground just north of Petersburg, Virginia. The 4th New Hampshire band was present when Grant attacked but failed to break the Confederate lines defending Petersburg on June 15-16, 1864. Bandleader Dignam's frustration over the prolongation of the war is revealed in a note he wrote at the end of a group of band arrangements he completed in August of 1864: "All these done either at Bermuda 100 or in front of Petersburg, Virginia during Grant's summer campaign, and most of it under the infernal fire of the Rebs. Hope before I score any more the -- -- -- -- (scratched out) cuss'd will be whipp'd or they will whip us or that the cuss'd thing'l bust. Eh how's that, eh?"

U.S. MARINE BAND

Francis M. Scala, Leader of the U.S. Marine Band from 1856 to 1871. Scala joined the ship's band of U.S.S. Brandywine at Naples in 1841. In 1848 he joined the Marine Band as an "E-flat Clarionett" player, becoming principal musician (bandleader) in 1856. The Marine Band at this time was made up largely of Europeans, many of them Italians. Courtesy U.S. Marine Corps Museum.

The United States Marine Band with a contingent of Marines in front of the Commandant's house, Marine Barracks, Washington, D.C., 1 April 1864. During the Civil War the Marine Band regularly performed at the White House. The instrumentation of the Marine Band under its wartime leader, Francis Scala, was similar to European bands of the period. In addition to a large woodwind section, the band had two French horns and four trombones. The trombone player pictured second from the right in the front row is Antonio Sousa, father of John Philip Sousa. Courtesy Library of Congress.

The United States Military Academy Band at West Point, 1864. This post band, which was officially established in 1816, would have been considered rather large for its day. Like the United States Marine Band, it boasted the luxury of having a fairly large woodwind section. Woodwind instruments generally were not used by regiment and brigade bands during the Civil War because they were prone to damage by extreme weather conditions and rough field use. A few slide trombones and French horns, also rarities in field bands, can be seen here as well. Courtesy West Point Library.

Louis Bentz and the dog Hans in the West Point Yearbook, 1865. Bentz is holding a B-flat keyed bugle, which by the time of the Civil War was no longer a standard band instrument. The keyed bugle was first introduced to America by West Point Bandmaster Richard Willis around 1815, and it became very popular. By the 1850s, it began to disappear from bands due to the rapid development of valved instruments. Old timers such as Bentz refused to learn to play the new instruments, however. Bentz enlisted as an army musician around 1835, shortly after he emigrated from his native Prussia, and served 40 years at the U.S. Military Academy as a musician in the band as well as a post bugler. He died on active duty in 1874 and is buried in the West Point Cemetery. No information is available on Hans' enlistment or musical abilities. Courtesy West Point Library.

Composite photograph of the 1st Brigade Band, 3rd Division, 15th Army Corps in 1864. Edwin O. Kimberly, leader, is pictured in the top left frame. Before the Civil War this band had been known as the Brodhead (Wisconsin) Silver Cornet Band. In July of 1861, the Brodhead Band enlisted with the 3rd Regiment Wisconsin Volunteers at Fond du Lac. A year later, the band was discharged from service along with most of the regimental bands in Federal service. After a lengthy period of reorganization, the band reenlisted in 1863, this time as a brigade band with the Army of Tennessee. The set of German silver OTS saxhorns pictured here, which cost $1,000.00, was manufactured by Allen & Hall of Boston in 1862. The part-books used by this band have survived and are housed in the Memorial Library of the University of Wisconsin at Madison. Courtesy Wisconsin Historical Society.

This rare composite is one of two known photos of Confederate bands. The Staunton (Virginia) Mountain Sax Horn Band was organized in 1855. In 1861 it enlisted with the 5th Virginia Infantry and served with the Stonewall Brigade through Appomattox. Their OTS saxhorns still exist today in the band hall of their direct descendants, The Stonewall Brigade Band of Staunton. Most are marked "Klemm & Bro, Philada" and were purchased by the band in 1859. An unusual feature of this band is the inclusion of flutist J.W. Alby. If a musician who played a non-brass instrument was a skilled performer, his talents might be used with the community's brass band. Courtesy Stonewall Brigade Band, Staunton, Virginia.

Regimental Band of the 26th North Carolina Troops, C.S.A., on furlough in July-August, 1862. The musicians are left to right: James M. Fisher (standing in for Alexander C. Meinung who was ill), Julius A. Leinbach, Daniel T. Crouse, Augustus L. Hauser, William H. Hall, Joe. O. Hall, A.P. Gibson, and bandleader Samuel T. Mickey. Courtesy Old Salem Restoration and the Moravian Music Foundation, Winston-Salem, North Carolina.

The bandsmen of the 26th North Carolina Regiment enlisted in the Confederate States Army in March of 1862 and served until 1865. Prior to the war, these Moravian musicians had been members of the Salem Brass Band. (Today, this band is the second oldest continuing musical organization in the United States.) Although small, the 26th North Carolina Band was considered one of the best bands in the Confederate Army. Colonel Zebulon Vance, commander of the 26th Regiment (and later Governor of North Carolina), and General Lee praised the band for their excellent music. The 26th North Carolina Band is the only Confederate band whose bandbooks have survived. Although some of their instruments were confiscated when the band was captured late in the war, the music stayed with the players and was taken back to Salem (now Winston-Salem) after their parole. The bandbooks are now in the collections of The Moravian Music Foundation. One of the part-books has a bullet hole in it (see below); its owner, Charlie Transou, narrowly escaped serious injury or death when the book was pierced by a minie ball in August of 1864.

Samuel T. Mickey, early 1860s. Mickey led the 26th North Carolina Band for more than three years during the Civil War while still in his mid-20s. His cornet is shown and described on the opposite page. Courtesy Old Salem Restoration and the Moravian Music Foundation, Winston-Salem.

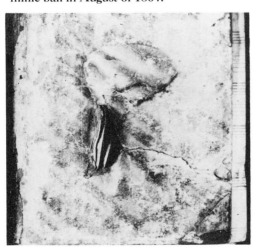

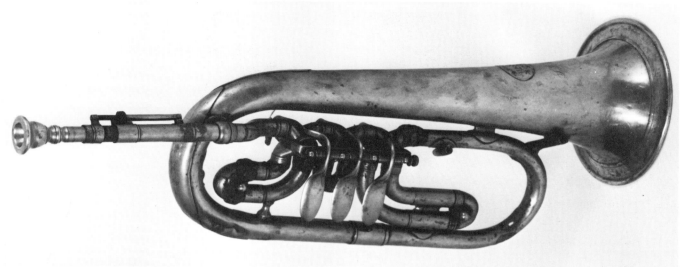

Sam Mickey's E-flat cornet with side action rotary valves. Marked "Manufactured by Allen Mfg. Co., 18 Harvard Pl., Boston," c. 1859. Courtesy Old Salem Restoration and the Moravian Music Foundation, Winston-Salem.

Lead E-flat cornet part to "Dixie and Bonnie Blue Flag." From the bandbooks of the 26th North Carolina Regiment Band. Courtesy the Moravian Music Foundation, Winston-Salem.

Samuel Mickey, c. 1890. Mickey is holding a cornet with Perinet piston valves. Courtesy Old Salem Restoration and the Moravian Music Foundation, Winston-Salem.

PORT ROYAL BAND

Regimental Band of the 3rd New Hampshire Volunteer Infantry, Port Royal, South Carolina, early 1862. This organization is probably the best documented Federal Army band, as its music books have survived and are in the Library of Congress and other archives. On July 31, 1861, Governor Berry of New Hampshire directed Gustavus W. Ingalls to "enlist twenty-four men as musicians" to be mustered into the service of the United States. Ingalls organized a band at Concord, and it was assigned to the 3rd New Hampshire Infantry. Although it was a field band of the volunteer army, it spent most of its one-year enlistment (August 1861 to August 1862) as a post band at Port Royal, Hilton Head, South Carolina. According to the historian of the 3rd New Hampshire Regiment: "The band was in demand for funerals and serenades. Its music drew tears and cheers. 'Twas an inspiration to all who stepped to its music, whether at dress parade or on the march." After regimental bands were mustered out in 1862, Ingalls and several former members of the 3rd New Hampshire band returned to Port Royal where they formed the nucleus of the 2nd Brigade Band of the 10th Corps. The instrumentation of the 3rd New Hampshire band as seen here in early 1862 is 16 OTS saxhorns, 1 piccolo, 2 clarinets and 4 percussion. The negro boy leaning on the bass drum is not a musician; he was a personal servant to bandmaster Ingalls. Ingalls is seated sixth from the left in the front row. Directly in front of him, seated on the drum, is Nathan M. Gove, the band's young drummer boy. Courtesy of the Library of Congress.

Right: Drummer boy Nathan Marcel Gove in 1861. Gove was born in Derry, New Hampshire on December 3, 1849. At the age of 11 he enlisted as a musician in the 3rd New Hampshire Volunteer Infantry and served with the regimental band at Port Royal until it was mustered out in 1862. Gove reenlisted with the 2nd Brigade Band, 10th Army Corps, in January of 1863 and returned to Port Royal where he served to the end of the war. In 1867 Gove joined the U.S. Navy and spent a year and a half as a 2nd class musician on the U.S.S. Franklin. He went to sea in hopes that the moist air would improve his health. (During his first army enlistment he had contracted malarial poisoning and never fully recovered from the disease.) In a letter to the U.S. Pension Office dated February 2, 1891, Gove wrote: "Entering the army at 11 years of age as drummer my service for nearly four years cost me my health and education, and changed the whole current of my life. I have never been well since." Gove died on October 1922, at the Michigan Soldier's Home, Grand Rapids. Authors' collection.

Left: Port Royal Bandbooks, 1861-62. These part-books are one of three sets of bandbooks used by the 3rd New Hampshire Regiment Band. (The other two sets are in the collections of the New Hampshire Historical Society and the New Hampshire Antiquarian Society.) Many of the approximately 136 selections contained in the bandbooks are by leading brass band composers and arrangers of the period—Claudio Grafulla, David Downing, Harvey Dodworth, Oscar Coon, J.P. King, and, of course, Gustavus Ingalls. Courtesy of the Library of Congress.

Camp scene of the 3rd New Hampshire Regiment Band, Port Royal, South Carolina, c. 1862. The musicians seated at the table are from left to right: Gustavus W. Ingalls, bandmaster; Samuel F. Brown, treasurer; and D. Arthur Brown, deputy bandmaster. Gustav Ingalls was 36 years old when he formed the 3rd New Hampshire band. Prior to 1861, he had achieved a high reputation as a conductor of brass bands and teacher of wind instruments. Both before and after the war, Ingalls was associated with several New England firms (including one of his own) that manufactured reed organs and other musical instruments. Courtesy of the Library of Congress.

Francis Harvey "Saxie" Pike, Drum Major, 2nd Brigade Band, 10th Army Corps, in 1864. Before the war, Saxie Pike was a member of the Manchester Cornet Band. (He was also a member of the fire company. Firemen were known as "saxies" in New York City and, apparently, elsewhere.) In 1861, Pike was drum major of the 2nd New Hampshire Regiment Band which accompanied the first Union troops through Baltimore after the 6th Massachusetts Infantry had been attacked by pro-Southern mobs. Reportedly, Pike proudly led his band down Pratt Street playing patriotic music (backed by enough troops to keep Baltimore citizens in line). Authors' collection.

Second Brigade Band, Tenth Army Corps, Hilton Head, South Carolina, 1864. Within six months after the 3rd New Hampshire Regiment Band was mustered out of service in August of 1862, its leader, Gustav Ingalls, organized a brigade band and returned to Port Royal, South Carolina. Ingalls' 2nd Brigade Band, which included approximately 20 percent of the musicians of his former band, was attached to Major General Gilmore's Headquarters, Department of the South. The band played at the ceremony to restore the U.S. flag to its former place of honor at Fort Sumter, April 14, 1865. The 2nd Brigade Band was mustered out of service on July 4, 1865. Drum major Saxie Pike can be seen in his bearskin hat at front and center of the band. Courtesy of the Boston Public Library.

HARVEY B. DODWORTH

The brothers Harvey and Allen Dodworth were members of a prominent musical family in New York City. In 1836 Thomas Dodworth, Sr. and his son Allen succeeded to the management of the National Band and soon afterward renamed it the Dodworth Band. In the early 1840s, Harvey became the leader of the Dodworth Band, a position he held for over 40 years. The Dodworths were skilled performers, prolific arrangers and composers, and musical entrepreneurs. In addition to managing a very successful band, which for many years had had a near monopoly of society music in New York City, the Dodworths owned a music store, published brass band music, ran a dancing academy, and operated a school for bandsmen; the latter reportedly trained 50 bandmasters and 500 bandsmen for the Union Army during the Civil War. They also were involved with the design and manufacture of brass instruments. By 1854 the Dodworth Band had achieved a national reputation for musical excellence. John Sullivan Dwight, a leading music critic of the era, wrote of the band that "brass instruments were never played with greater delicacy or refinement." The band could function as a cornet band, as a reed-brass band, or as an orchestra. In 1861 Harvey Dodworth and his band served with the 71st New York State Militia. During their three-month enlistment, the bandsmen were first stationed at the Navy Yard in Washington where they regularly gave concerts. The band served with the 71st Regiment at the Battle of Bull Run (First Manassas). For more than two decades after the war, the Dodworth Band remained one of the best musical organizations in the country.

Harvey B. Dodworth (1821-1891), virtuoso cornetist and leader of the Dodworth Band of New York City. His five valve OTS saxhorn is shown and described below. Oil painting by Charles Waldo Jenkins, 1857. Courtesy The New York Historical Society.

Soprano saxhorn in A-flat. Marked "Made by J. Lathrop Allen, 17 Harvard Pl., Boston, for H.B. Dodworth, N.Y.," c. 1855. German silver with five Allen rotary valves. From the Collections of the Henry Ford Museum and Greenfield Village, Dearborn, Michigan. The design of this unusual instrument probably was suggested by Harvey Dodworth. The three top valves are played with the right hand in the usual manner; the loops for these valves are proportioned to fit the overall tube length which is pitched in A-flat (a perfect fourth higher than the E-flat soprano saxhorn). The two side valves, which are played with the left hand, lower the overall pitch of the instrument to F and E-flat respectively. This instrument probably was designed for ease in high register playing and for better intonation. Apparently the instrument was not too successful because the design was not widely copied.

Rope tension bass drum, c. 1836. According to Harvey Dodworth's son, this bass drum was played at 10 different Presidential inauguration ceremonies and at the Battle of Bull Run where it was abandoned and later retrieved. Courtesy The New York Historical Society.

Allen Dodworth, author of *Dodworth's Brass Band School,* is depicted on this piano sheet music cover to the "Allen Polka" by Elbert Anderson (New York, Wm. Hall & Son, 1850). Courtesy Kurt Stein.

The back cover of *Dodworth's Brass Band School* (1853) illustrates the many facets of the Dodworth family business.

CLAUDIO S. GRAFULLA

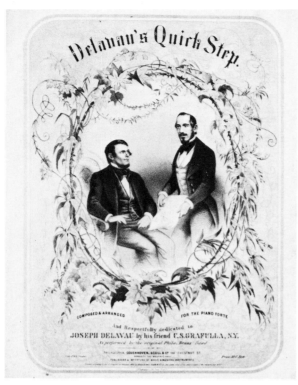

Claudio S. Grafulla was a first-rate composer of military and popular music and an outstanding Civil War era bandleader. Grafulla was born on the Spanish island of Menorca in 1810. Soon after he came to America in 1838, he played in Ned Lothian's New York Brass Band. (This band was attached to the 7th Regiment New York State Militia.) By 1850 Grafulla had achieved a national reputation as a composer of military band music. His excellent compositions and arrangements appear in most surviving bandbooks of the period. A thoroughly trained musician with a natural aptitude for conducting, Grafulla organized his own band in 1860. Grafulla employed trombones and a fairly large woodwind section in his 48-piece band. Because Grafulla's superb ensemble was formed to replace the old band of the 7th Regiment, his organization was popularly known as the 7th Regiment Band. In 1861 Grafulla and his musicians went to war with the 7th Regiment and served for three months. After their discharge, the band continued to support the war effort by giving benefit concerts at home. Grafulla led the 7th Regiment Band until his death in 1880. An obituary notice in the New York Times extolled Grafulla's leadership of the 7th Regiment Band and noted his important contribution to the musical life of New York City and the nation.

Piano sheet music cover showing Claudio Grafulla (right) presenting an original quickstep march, composed in 1852, to Joseph Delavau. Courtesy of Kurt Stein.

The lead E-flat cornet part to the "Drum Corps or 7th Regiment Quickstep" by Claudio S. Grafulla. From the Port Royal Bandbooks at the Library of Congress.

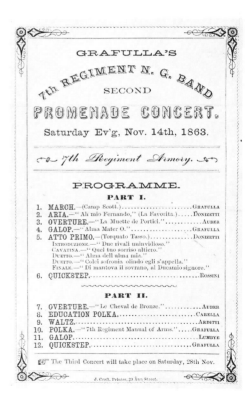

Handbill announcing a concert by the 7th Regiment Band that was given in 1863.

The 7th Regiment New York State Militia at Camp Worth (Kingston), July 1855. The 7th Regiment Band, which is pictured in the center along with the Drum Corps, is playing while the troops are forming for a review and inspection. Lithograph by Thomas Benecke from an original painting by Major Otto Boetticher. Courtesy of Kurt Stein.

PATRICK S. GILMORE

Opposite: Gilmore's Band with a contingent of militia, c. 1872. The emblem on the bandsmen's hats reads "Gilmore's Band." The musician standing to the right of the bass drum (behind the seated boy) probably is Matthew Arbuckle, Gilmore's solo cornetist. Apparently, Gilmore was not present when the photograph was taken. Courtesy Henry Deeks.

Patrick Gilmore in 1856. Courtesy M. Wesley Marans.

Patrick Gilmore (seated second from the left) with the members of his 22nd Regiment Band, c. 1880s. Courtesy of the American Bandmasters Association Library, Special Collections in Music, University of Maryland.

Patrick Sarsfield Gilmore was one of the most famous bandleaders and musical impresarios in American history. He was born in County Galway, Ireland, on Christmas day in 1829. At the age of 18, he joined a military band which was stationed in Canada. After a year in the service, he quit the military and moved to Boston where he quickly established a reputation as a gifted cornetist. At age 22, Gilmore was appointed leader of the Boston Brass Band, one of the best musical organizations in New England. (From the date of its formation in 1835, the Boston Brass Band had only been led by virtuoso keyed buglers—Edward (Ned) Kendall, Joseph Green, and Eben Flagg.) After three successful years with the Boston Brass Band, Gilmore moved to Salem where he was director of the Salem Brass Band, a position he held for five years. In 1859 Gilmore was invited back to Boston to direct the Boston Brigade Band, which was experiencing difficulties. With his usual energy and enthusiasm, Gilmore revitalized the organization and changed its name to his own. Gilmore's Band was similar to the Dodworth organization in that it was a large, flexible ensemble capable of providing music for almost any occasion. From 1859 to 1863, Gilmore was co-owner of a Boston music store that sold band instruments—Gilmore & Russell. Later he was part owner in two instrument manufacturing firms—Gilmore, Graves & Co. (1864-66) and Wright, Gilmore & Co. (1867-68).

In October of 1861, Gilmore and his band enlisted with the 24th Massachusetts Volunteer Infantry. The bandmen served with General Burnside in North Carolina until their discharge in August of 1862. Upon returning home, Gilmore gave concerts with his band and devoted much time to reorganizing militia and army bands. Following the war, Gilmore organized two mammoth musical extravaganzas in Boston (1869 and 1872) that received national and international attention. From 1873 until the time of his death in 1892, Gilmore directed the superb 22nd Regiment Band of New York (also known as Gilmore's Band). This large ensemble of some 65 musicians, which toured the nation and the world, set a pattern of instrumentation and a standard of musical performance that were emulated by many professional bands in the 1890s and early twentieth century.

EPILOGUE

HOW TO ORGANIZE A BRASS BAND
by
George F. Patton

"In view of the fact that this volume may fall into the hands of many, who, though not actually members of an active Band may yet feel an interest in the various questions concerned in the formation and management of one. . . .

"It is a fact not to be denied that the existence of a good Brass Band in any town or community is at once an indication of enterprise among its people, and an evidence that a certain spirit of taste and refinement pervades the masses, for though the people at large do not actually keep up the Band, they can yet exert a most important influence toward deciding its success or failure, by means of the interest they take in it, and the amount of encouragement they extend toward its members. No institution can thrive in a community where it is not appreciated, and therefore when we see a town with flourishing public enterprises, such as news-papers, schools, libraries, picture galleries, literary and scientific societies, concert halls, theaters, *Brass Bands* etc., we need not be told that it is the dwelling place of intelligent and cultivated people, for in all these institutions supported by its inhabitants we recognize the unfailing indication of culture and refinement. . . .

"So to all young friends who may feel an inclination to become members of a good band, or to aid in establishing one, the Author has this to say,—go ahead with your whole energy, heart, head and soul. . . .

"We now come to the question of how to get up a new Band. . . .

"As Professionals need no advice on this point it is to be understood that the suggestions about to be offered refer particularly to Amateurs.

"First comes the selection of men. As a rule, it is well here to avoid taking in fellows who 'play by ear,' that is, if they belong to that numerous class, who, having naturally more or less musical talent, have yet been too idle to improve it by study. . . . Such fellows besides being often dissipated, are most always vain and idle, and if so will only prove stumbling blocks in the way of the Band. Still, there are many persons who play 'by ear' without possessing any of these disagreeable attributes of vanity, idleness, dissipated habits etc., and in that case are in every way eligible as members, and will often prove very valuable acquisitions to a Band. The most essential requisite is that a man should be *patient* and *teachable*.

"As a rule however, it is better to take simple, honest fellows who do not know a note of music, but who bid fair to be patient under instruction; and who having no consciousness of talent are not likely to develop that spirit of self conceit, which gives so much trouble to a teacher in the case of a fellow, who, imagining that he knows something already, holds himself as a superior, and snubs his more ignorant companions, who in their turn get to hate him cordially.

"Having selected the men, pick out the most intelligent and ambitious of the lot for Cornet players, and if they are a little young, so much the better, for beyond a certain age a man learns music only with difficulty, and his fingers and tongue are apt to remain more or less clumsy about the execution of rapid solos. The next most important place to be filled is that of the Tuba player. He should be a moderately stout fellow, capable of supporting the 'big horn' without getting tired, and besides having plenty of good common sense, his supply of patience should be practically inexhaustible, for in practising accompaniment parts with beginners a Tuba player, who has not the qualities of patience and good humor is likely to get disgusted, and if a man of profane habits is apt to swear in a disagreeable way at the stupid blunders made by his companions of the Althorns [sic] and Tenors, and this tends to make them angry in turn, and the disgust and swearing may become mutual, and so little private feuds spring up which will eventually undermine the Band.

"For the Side instruments and Drums it does not make so much difference, except perhaps in the case of the Small Drum player who as a matter of preference should be a sprightly young fellow with some little idea of drum playing already, and a pretty good natural idea of music generally. There are numbers of such boys to be found everywhere, and they can be easily taught to play by note.

"If in a new Band there is to be a Baritone or Solo Alto, it is necessary to entrust them to men of intelligence and ambition, just as with the Cornets, for to an absolute beginner the former are even more difficult to manage than the latter. . . .

"To Amateurs the Author has also this piece of advice to offer. Do not let anybody persuade you to bother with Piccolos, Clarinets and Slide Trombones. The common Band instruments with three valves are the easiest to learn, and sound just as well as any, and in the hands of inexperienced musicians better in fact than any other. . . ." (G.F. Patton, *A Practical Guide to the Arrangement of Band Music* [New York: John F. Stratton & Co., 1875], pp. 175-77.)

DISCOGRAPHY

Part I below is a chronological listing of recordings of Civil War era brass band music played on *period* instruments. All of the albums are highly recommended and unless noted otherwise all are available. There is very little duplication of music on these recordings.

Part II includes recordings of brass band music played on *modern* instruments. These albums are noteworthy because they contain good notes and because it is instructive to compare the sound of modern instruments to period instruments; the sound is quite different.

PART I

The Civil War: Its Music and Its Sounds. Eastman Wind Ensemble, Frederick Fennell, conductor. 2 vols. Mercury Records LPS2-501 (2 discs) and LPS2-502 (2 discs), (1961 and 1963). Good historical notes by the conductor. Period instruments are from public and private museums and private collections. Although these historically important recordings are no longer available, most of the music has been reissued in a one-volume album (two discs) titled *Music of the Civil War* (Mercury Golden Import SRI-77011).

19th-Century American Ballroom Music: Waltzes, Marches, Polkas & Other Dances (1840-1860). Smithsonian Social Orchestra & Quadrille Band. James Weaver, director. Nonesuch Records H-71313 (1975). Good program notes by Cynthia Hoover. This album is an outgrowth of a concert given in Washington, D.C., on March 11, 1974. Musicians are from the National Symphony Orchestra and other leading Washington ensembles. Period instruments are from the Smithsonian Institution and other collections.

Our Musical Past: A Concert for Brass Band, Voice & Piano. Frederick Fennell, director. Library of Congress OMP 101-102 (2 discs), (1976). Available from the Recorded Sound Section, Music Division, Library of Congress, Washington, D.C., 20540. Excellent scholarly notes by Jon Newsom, Assistant Chief, Music Division, Library of Congress. This recording is an outgrowth of a concert given at the Library of Congress on Sept. 27, 1974. Musicians are from the National Symphony Orchestra and other Washington ensembles. Period instruments are from the Smithsonian Institution and other collections.

Military Band Music of the Confederacy. Heritage Americana Cornet-Saxhorn Brass Band. Robert Garofalo, conductor. Military Music in America, Vol. 5, The Company of Military Historians, Washington, D.C. (1979). Historical notes by Mark Elrod and Robert Garofalo. Period instruments are from the Elrod Collection.

American Brass Quintet Playing Music of the mid:1800s on Instruments of the Period. Titanic Records Ti-81 (1980). Notes by H. Wiley Hitchcock and Robert Rosenbaum. This recording is an outgrowth of a concert given in May of 1980 to commemorate the opening of the American Wing of the Metropolitan Museum of Art, New York City. Instruments are from the Rosenbaum Collection.

The Yankee Brass Band: Music from Mid-Nineteenth Century America. The American Brass Quintet Brass Band. New World Records NW 312 Stereo (1981). Excellent historical notes by Jon Newsom and Robert Sheldon. Period instruments are from the collections of The Metropolitan Museum of Art, Dorothy and Robert Rosenbaum, and others.

Battle Cry of Freedom: Military Music of Union Army Bands. Performed on original Civil War instruments by Heritage Americana Cornet-Saxhorn Brass Band. Robert Garofalo, conductor. Produced by Heritage Americana, Inc., Washington, D.C. (1982). Historical notes by Mark Elrod, Robert Garofalo, and George Wheelock. Period instruments are from the Elrod Collection.

PART II

Homespun America: Marches, Waltzes, Polkas & Serenades; Music of the Social Orchestra; Songs of the 19th Century. Eastman Wind Ensemble and Eastman Chorale. Donald Hunsberger and Robert DeCormier, Directors. Vox SVBX 5309 (3 discs), (1976). Music of the Manchester Cornet Band (Walter Dignam Collection) played on modern instruments. Excellent notes by Donald Hunsberger.

The American Brass Band Journal (1853). The Empire Brass Quintet and Friends. Columbia Masterworks M34192 (1976). Notes by Jon Newsom.

American Brass Band Journal Revisited. Empire Brass Quintet and Friends. Frederick Fennell, conductor. Sine Qua Non Productions SAS-2017 (1978). Notes by Jon Newsom. The title of this album is misleading; the music is from the *Stratton Military Band Journal* and not the *Brass Band Journal*.

BIBLIOGRAPHY

Baines, Anthony, *Brass Instruments: Their History and Development*. New York: Charles Scribner's Sons, 1981.

Brice, Marshall M., *The Stonewall Brigade Band*. Verona, Virginia: McClure Printing Co., 1967.

Bufkin, William A., *Union Bands of the Civil War (1862-1865): Instrumentation and Score Analysis*. Unpublished Ph.D. dissertation, The Louisiana State University, 1973.

Cipolla, Frank J., "Annotated Guide for the Study and Performance of Nineteenth Century Band Music in the United States," *Journal of Band Research*, Vol. 14, No. 1, Fall 1978, pp. 22-40.

Dudgeon, Ralph Thomas, *The Keyed Bugle, Its History, Literature and Technique*. Unpublished Ph.D. dissertation, University of California, San Diego, 1980.

Eliason, Robert E., *Early American Brass Makers*. Nashville: The Brass Press, 1979.

_____, *Graves and Company Musical Instrument Makers*. Dearborn, Michigan: The Edison Institute, 1975.

_____, *Keyed Bugles in the United States*. Washington: Smithsonian Institution Press, 1972.

Fennell, Frederick, "The Civil War: Its Music and its Sounds," *Journal of Band Research*," Vol. 4, No. 2, Spring 1968, pp. 36-44; Vol. 5, No. 1, Fall 1968, pp. 8-14.

Garofalo, Robert and Elrod, Mark, *Heritage Americana: A Unique Collection of American Civil War Military Brass Band Music*. Edited for modern brass ensemble with historical annotations. San Diego: Kjos Music Company, 1981.

_____, "Heritage Americana: Reflections on the Performance Practices of Mid-Nineteenth Century Brass Bands," *Journal of Band Research*, Vol. 17, No. 1, Fall 1981, pp. 1-26.

Hall, Harry H., *A Johnny Reb Band from Salem: The Pride of Tarheelia*. Raleigh: The North Carolina Confederate Centennial Commission, 1963.

Hutchinson, Thomas, *The American Musical Directory, 1861*. New York: Da Capo Press [Music Reprint Series], 1980.

Newsom, Jon, "The American Brass Band Movement," *The Quarterly Journal of the Library of Congress*, Vol. 36, No. 2, Spring 1979, pp. 115-139.

Olson, Kenneth E., *Music and Musket: Bands and Bandsmen of the American Civil War*. Westport, Connecticut: Greenwood Press, 1981.

Schwartz, Harry W., *Bands of America*. New York: Doubleday and Co., 1957.

White, William C., *A History of Military Music in America*. Westport, Connecticut: Greenwood Press, 1975.

Wise, Arthur and Lord, Francis A., *Bands and Drummer Boys of the Civil War*. South Brunswick, N.J.: Thomas Yoseloff, 1966.

INDEX

ABOUT THE AUTHORS

ROBERT GAROFALO

MARK ELROD

Robert Garofalo is Professor of Music and Conductor of Wind Ensembles at the School of Music, The Catholic University of America, Washington, D.C. He is a graduate of Mansfield University. After additional studies at the Eastman School of Music, he joined the United States Air Force Band in Washington and toured widely with its jazz ensemble, the Airmen of Note. His master's degree and his doctorate in musicology were earned at Catholic University. Garofalo is the author of many books, articles, and music publications in the fields of instrumental music performance, pedagogy, and history. He is the conductor of Heritage Americana and has recorded two authoritative albums of Civil War military brass band music. He resides in College Park, Maryland, with his wife, Ann, and their two children, Michael and Robin. Photograph by G. Thaddeus Jones.

Mark Elrod, a native of the Washington, D.C. area, graduated from Valley Forge Military Academy and Salem College. He served with the United States Army in South Vietnam and later was stationed at Fort Myer, Virginia, where he performed with The Old Guard Fife and Drum Corps. He later was research and special projects NCO with the United States Marine Band in Washington. He is now on active duty with the National Guard. Elrod is an authority on nineteenth century American bands, instruments, and music. His collections include one of the country's largest private holdings of Civil War era band music and musical instruments. He is an elected Fellow of the Company of Military Historians. He lives in Gaithersburg, Maryland, with his wife, Judy. Photograph by G. Thaddeus Jones.

ABOUT HERITAGE AMERICANA

Heritage Americana Band (pictured on the back cover) is an independent musical organization whose members are dedicated to the performance of Civil War era brass band music on period instruments—cornets, saxhorns, rope tension drums, and so on. The performers are professional musicians and military bandsmen from the Washington, D.C. area. The group was founded by Robert Garofalo and Mark Elrod in 1978 as the performance arm of Heritage Americana, Inc., a nonprofit research-performance project. During the past several years, Heritage Americana has conducted two East Coast tours and given more than 50 concerts, lectures, and demonstrations at conferences, conventions, museums, state and national parks, and places of historical interest. In addition, Heritage Americana has recorded two Civil War albums and published a collection of mid-nineteenth century brass band music edited for modern brass ensemble. Photograph by Peter Patrone.